MW00737524

H I S
Awesome
M A J E S T Y

HIS
Awesome
MAJESTY

Praising God's Greatness

JO HUDDLESTON

His Awesome Majesty: Praising God's Greatness
copyright © 1997 Jo Huddleston

Published by Hendrickson Publishers
P.O. Box 3473
Peabody, Massachusetts 01961-3473

All rights reserved. Except for brief quotations in printed reviews, no part of this publication may be reproduced, stored in a retrieval system, or transmitted in any form or by any means (printed, written, photocopied, visual electronic, audio or otherwise) without prior permission of the publisher.

Printed in the United States of America

ISBN 1-56563-299-0

First printing—August 1997

Unless otherwise noted, all Scripture references in this book are taken from the Holy Bible: New International Version, copyright 1973, 1978, 1984 by the International Bible Society.

Scripture references marked TLB are taken from The Living Bible, copyright 1971 by Tyndale House Publishers.

Scripture references marked NKJV are taken from the Holy Bible, New King James Version, copyright 1984 by Thomas Nelson, Inc.

Cover design by Paetzold Design, Batavia, Ill.
Interior design by Pinpoint Marketing, Kirkland, Wash.
Edited by Judy Bodmer and Heather Stroobosscher

Library of Congress Cataloging-in-Publication Data

Huddleston, Jo, 1935–
    His awesome majesty: praising God's greatness / Jo Huddleston
        p. cm.
    ISBN 1-56563-299-0 (cloth)
    1. Praise of God—Meditations. 2. God—Worship and love—
        Meditations.   I. Title.
8V4817.H83   1997   97-28488
242—dc21   CIP

Contents

Introduction

God affirms his greatness in every aspect of life. He gives us sunrises and sunsets; babies and children. God gives us family and friends; joy and innocence. But his greatest gift is his Son Jesus Christ, in whose name we may praise God.

It is my hope that reading this book will help you focus not on your problems but on praising God for his promised comfort and encouragement. May these meditations guide you to a harvest of God's blessings, giving you a spiritual tonic for hope-filled living.

As you read, I trust you will feel the caress of God's healing words and wear a garment of praise, not a spirit of despair (Isa. 61:3). Allow this book to cut a wide spiritual path across Satan's mine fields in your life, clearing the way for personal access to God's power.

Remember that God comes in our suffering and during our happiness, but always . . .

God comes in awesome majesty (Job 37:22).

1

PERSPECTIVE

Perspective

FINDING GOD IN YOUR CIRCUMSTANCES

I folded laundry and straightened up the house before falling exhausted into bed. I looked forward to having a head start on tomorrow's chores so I could meet a friend for lunch. But so much for planning ahead!

After being the short-order cook for breakfast and preparing lunches for picky eaters, I could hardly recognize my kitchen. Getting everyone dressed and out the door on time left the house looking like a whirlwind had passed through.

Why do they call them *new* days when each day is a repeat of the one before? Finished housework becomes unfinished, only to do again!

When morning's light creeps over the horizon, the new day claims the attention of most living creatures. For the rooster, each dawn provides another opportunity to flap his wings and announce the new day's arrival. But for the weary person who worked the night shift or the one who lost sleep tending a sick child, the new day presents a drudgery to be tackled with a tired mind and body.

A visit to the doctor may reveal the impending miracle of birth or the discovery of a life-threatening illness. A telegram can bring good news or bad. The same playing field produces victory and defeat.

We assign relative importance to our circumstances. Whatever judgment we conclude, in every situation the purposes of God are at work: "In all things God works for the good of those who love him, who have been called according to his purpose" (Rom. 8:28).

God was present as Moses led the Israelites out of Egyptian bondage (Exod. 3:7–10) and while they wandered forty years in the wilderness (Num. 32:13). God remained with the Israelites when they escaped from their captors across the Red Sea on a dry ocean floor which he provided (Exod. 14).

God's presence was with Daniel when King Darius appointed him to his royal staff. God was also with Daniel when the king condemned him to the den of lions (Dan. 6). God's purposes were at work when the impulsive Peter denied knowing Jesus (John 18) and also when Jesus personally restored Peter (John 21).

Perhaps in their suffering and trials, Moses, Daniel, and Peter wondered at God's purposes. Surely in their times of deepest need, these faithful saints thought God had distanced himself from their circumstance. Not so.

Over and over God proved his universal presence, not only for these three servants but for countless others. God holds the power of omnipresence (Jer. 23:23–24).

Maybe we won't be privileged to see God's presence in a blinding light as did the apostle Paul on the Damascus road (Acts 9:3–4) or hear God speak from a burning bush (Exod. 3:4). But God's presence prevails everywhere and in everything. God inhabits the ordinary and transforms its character into extraordinary. When we learn to trust him, God works this miracle of change in us. He will enable us to step beyond our abilities and climb above our circumstances.

Whatever our crisis or celebration, our boredom or adventure, God is present. He is there working out his purpose in each life. We cannot conceal ourselves from him (Ps. 139:7–12).

To find God sometimes requires a change in the attitude of our heart. Choosing not to concentrate on our problems but instead searching for God's available power, we will become dependent on God rather than on ourselves for solutions. Such an attitude will flavor our daily behavior and strengthen our faith to endure the bad times. From this perspective will come our admission of the reality of God's presence.

Are you wandering in a wilderness like the Israelites? Does every bump in the road steer you off course? If so, draw God closer into your life. Woodrow Wilson said, "Without God the world would be a maze without a clue."

I pray that the following selections will help you to look for God in your circumstances. You can find him, for he's already there. Acknowledging God's presence will help you to see all things in his proper perspective.

SELLING CARS AND SENSING GOD

For from him and through him and to him are all things. To him be the glory forever! (Romans 11:36)

I sat in my car at a busy intersection, waiting for the traffic light to change from red to green. As I watched cars pass in front of me from the left and from the right, some waving balloons of red, green, and yellow caught my eye.

They were part of a marketing scheme. A local car dealer had attached dozens of them to automobiles, hoping to draw attention to what he was selling.

And so my gaze went from the balloons to the shiny cars as I waited in traffic. A blustery wind gusted through the area, swinging balloons in all directions. Their strings strained against the wind. Suddenly one bunch broke free.

Once part of a colorful collage among automobiles and people, these floated upward. I watched their journey as they rose against the cloudless blue sky until out of sight. Just as I had earlier allowed the balloons to draw my attention to their surroundings, I did so again. But this time, instead of looking at cars and salespeople, I saw the immense sky.

I sensed the enormity of creation and the presence of God. At an ordinary intersection on an ordinary day, I was blessed with definite assurance of God's nearness.

One bunch of balloons, two viewpoints. The car dealer had planned for the balloons to point people to the automobiles. God used them to bring himself closer into at least one life.

Praise the LORD. Praise God in his sanctuary; praise him in his mighty heavens. (Psalm 150:1)

We Can't Change Yesterday

Don't brag about being wise and good if you are bitter.
(James 3:14 TLB)

The lines of my friend's constant frown creased his brow. His eyes held no brightness as he spoke about his latest setback. Sliding low in his chair, he asked, "How can you be so positive all the time?"

"It's a decision I made a long time ago," I replied.

"Well, if you'd been passed over again for a promotion, I guess you wouldn't be so cheery."

"Maybe not for a while," I said. "But I'd try to allow God to work out his plans for my life."

"Those guys upstairs don't want to see me get ahead. They've just got it in for me," he announced, and slammed his fist into his other hand.

Life has dealt my friend many hardships. Now, his unforgiving spirit won't release its tight grip on deep-seated grudges. His resulting bitterness about past wrongs hinders his joy in daily relationships.

We are all familiar with the worldly quality of bitterness. Ill will against hostilities collects; brooding over being wronged begins. Then, resentment sprouts, spawning grudges. This domino effect finally produces the poison of bitterness which breaks hearts and relationships, just as with my friend.

The preacher in Hebrews urges us to "make every effort to live in peace . . . that no bitter root grows up to cause trouble" (Heb. 12:14–15). Paul urges the Christians at Colosse to "bear with each other and forgive whatever grievances you may have against one another. . . . Let the peace of Christ rule in your hearts" (Col. 3:13, 15).

We can neutralize bitterness by wrapping a blanket of God's love around those we feel have wronged us. Forgiveness can break the bonds of bitterness.

We can't change anything about our yesterdays. But we don't have to cling to their bad memories. We don't have to remain captive to bitterness. Instead, we can try to "be kind and compassionate to one another, forgiving each other, just as in Christ God forgave you" (Eph. 4:32).

We can release our bitterness and replace it with forgiveness. God's love will help us forgive one another, restoring broken relationships.

Praise the LORD. Give thanks to the LORD, for he is good; his love endures forever. (Psalm 106:1)

Microwave Solutions

But if we hope for what we do not yet have, we wait for it patiently. (Romans 8:25)

I had watched the man as he hurried his grocery buggy from aisle to aisle. Now, as we both waited in the check-out line, he looked down the row of cashiers. When one line would shorten, he'd steer his buggy to it. Then when a price check slowed progress, he'd change lines again. I could see his lips move as he grumbled under his breath and finally spoke out loud.

"Don't they know they need more workers here?" he said loudly enough for all to hear. He threw his hands toward the ceiling. Pushing his buggy aside, he stormed out of the store.

Do you ever notice people in morning church services who begin to look at their watches impatiently around 11:45 A.M.? They seem so anxious for the service to end.

The gaily wrapped red and green packages, lying dormant under the Christmas tree, tempt children to impatience. Restless young people can't wait to move out of their homes. Young parents become frustrated at the behavior of their small children. Older adults show intolerance toward their aging parents. Each of these characterizes our instant-satisfaction society.

When we are impatient, we are also intolerant. Sometimes our selfish desires demand microwave-type solutions.

The Bible offers examples of impatience and its negative results. Remember the parable of the prodigal son (Luke 15:11–32)? Beyond the lesson of his wasteful spending lies a message concerning his impatience. This son demanded his inheritance, to spend as he chose. When he'd wasted all of his money on short-term pleasures, he learned about genuine want.

In contrast, we read about the farmer who plants expectantly and waits for the fruits of his labor (James 5:7–8). This scripture encourages us to be patient like the farmer.

Paul urges us to "be patient with everyone" (1 Thess. 5:14). And, again, he implores us to be "patient in affliction" (Rom. 12:12). Scripture also teaches that God's promises will be inherited by those who embrace patience (Heb. 6:11–12).

Planting the word "wait" into daily living weakens the weed of impatience and allows the blossom of perseverance.

When I was pregnant with my first child, I anticipated the delivery time to the extent of aggravating those around me. I wanted to do this child-birthing thing exactly by all the books I'd read. When contractions were five minutes apart, I became anxious to rush to the hospital, even though it was located only two blocks away.

Finally, we braved the January cold for our short car ride and the nurses settled me into the labor room. And then we waited. Impatience claimed no honor that night. Only when the baby was ready was it delivered.

I try to benefit from that memory when I wait for God to answer my prayers. My selfish timetable rarely coincides with God's. But he does answer prayer, according to his will; the problem of impatience rests with me.

Selfish impatience serves no good purpose. Instead, we're to pursue endurance; wait expectantly, believing in results; and be long-suffering in tribulation.

How and where do we find forbearance? From God. He is the author of patience and will grant it to us (Rom. 15:5).

I will praise your name, O LORD, for it is good. (Psalm 54:6)

Housecleaning in the Heart

Above all else, guard your heart, for it is the wellspring of life. (Proverbs 4:23)

One summer day, my husband and my seventeen-year-old son worked all afternoon to underpin the deck. Typically, these two never walk away from an unfinished task. But today they put away their materials and tools before completing the project. They entered the cool kitchen in silence.

"Are you finished?" I asked.

"No, not yet," my son answered. "We can't figure out how to fit the corner. We decided to wait and ask the salesman at the lumber store what we need to do. We'll get it right tomorrow."

Apparently discarding all worry, my son had worked through his obvious frustrations. With a positive outlook toward the unsolved problem, he was willing to tackle it tomorrow.

Scripture teaches that the heart produces the words we speak and the attitude we maintain (Matt. 12:34–35; 15:18–19). Diligence is necessary in the housekeeping of our heart, because what starts from within will affect every aspect of our life (Prov. 4:23). Therefore, in order to live a positive life, we must first nurture that lifestyle in our mind and heart.

We need to continually clear out the dust balls of negative thoughts, replacing them with wholesome thinking on things which are true, noble, right, pure, lovely, and admirable (Phil. 4:8). We can live our life in a more positive way when we develop our attitude with words and thoughts pleasing to God (Ps. 19:14).

I will sing to the LORD all my life; I will sing praise to my God as long as I live. (Psalm 104:33)

Rescue Granted

The Lord lifts up those who are bowed down. (Psalm 146:8)

"**M**other! What is this?"

My daughter's words stabbed through the semi-darkness into my sleepless rest. I bolted from my narrow cot next to her hospital bed. Carrying twins had taken its toll on her body. Her hormone levels had zoomed, causing her "morning sickness" to last all day, every day. The doctors ordered glucose administered by intravenously to restore her strength and improve the environment for the developing babies.

Now, propped up on one feeble elbow, she stared at her bed, cringing against the safety railing behind her. In the dim spray of a night-light, I discovered that somehow one of the colorful connections in the clear tube snaking from her arm to the overhead bag had separated. The growing dark spot on the bed wasn't leaking glucose, but her blood.

When the connection had been pulled apart and no glucose coursed its way down the tubing into her vein, the blood had begun to flow from her body onto the stark white sheet.

I fumbled for the nurse's call button, dreading how long it might take. Instinct screamed that for the next precious moments only I could stop the loss of my daughter's blood and whatever strength she had regained. I reached for the i.v. tubing with steady hands. Grasping it at a point near her arm, I crimped it between my thumb and forefinger. Gratitude shone in her eyes as she rested her head on the pillow. She seemed confident that I could rescue her from this emergency.

"Yes, may I help you?" In the half-light of that hospital room, the voice from the box on the wall granted rescue for my daughter's life.

Seconds later a nurse rushed into the room, flipping on the bright overhead light and assessing the situation. With experienced hands, she repaired the broken connection.

I watched as the red in the tube near my daughter's arm paled. The glucose made its way through the tubing and pushed her blood back into her body where it belonged. Soon the tubing again flowed with the clear, healing liquid.

When the crisis was over, my daughter resting again on clean linens, I willed my eyes not to close as I lay on the tiny cot for the rest of the night. I decided to keep a closer vigil.

Reflecting on that incident, I wonder how I reacted with such calm. My daughter, too, had seemed secure, lying back quietly the instant she saw me come to stand beside her.

I'm convinced the prevailing calm that night resulted from God's presence. He guided my thoughts and my hands. He gave my daughter a peaceful patience while the nurse worked.

When we base our life's foundation on God, we won't have to hesitate in crisis situations, searching for him and his help before we act. We can rest on his promises and react with calm assurance that he is our ever-present defense through every difficulty.

Praise him for his acts of power; praise him for his surpassing greatness. (Psalm 150:2)

CREAKING DOORS

So do not fear, for I am with you. (Isaiah 41:10)

Before television, when I was about ten years old, my family joined around the radio for a weekly program called *Inner Sanctum.* Each scary episode invaded our home with sounds of the gradual opening of a creaking door. After thirty suspenseful minutes, that same creaking door slowly slammed shut, cementing frightful mental images.

For many years, remembering that program caused me paralyzing panic in the dark. And, even today, I oil creaking doors as soon as possible; I don't want reminders of that haunting radio program.

The fear that show caused me most of my life didn't come from anything that could actually harm me. My fear, although real to me, came from anticipated danger which could not touch me. I transferred fictional happenings from radio onto myself and, therefore, terror in the dark became a reality.

What creaking doors do we face daily? Fear of thunderstorms, eating alone, speaking before people, that first day on the new job, or walking alone into a new school? Of course, those can be fearful times—but only in our minds, not usually bringing physical danger.

Fear does not come from God. He gives, instead, a spirit of power and love (2 Tim. 1:7). God is perfect love that can banish fear (1 John 4:18).

Fear is a human quality. It's expressing doubt about God's presence with us in times of supposed or real danger. Instead, God wants us to be powerful in love.

Just as I stop creaking doors with oil, we can enlist faith in God as our help and shield in the face of fear (Ps.115:11).

*For the LORD your God is God of gods and Lord of lords,
the great God, mighty and awesome. (Deuteronomy 10:17)*

Winning Blueprint

*Do not be anxious about anything, but in everything, by
prayer and petition, with thanksgiving, present your requests
to God. And the peace of God, which transcends all understanding, will guard your hearts and your minds in Christ
Jesus. (Philippians 4:6–7)*

My neighbors had budgeted successfully toward a much
needed vacation. The day before they were to leave,
their car broke down, and estimates to repair it were a few
hundred dollars. With just enough money in hand to cover the
vacation expenses, what would they do about the car? How
could they not have disappointment and frustration?

"I'm thankful God has allowed us to have some savings,"
my neighbor said. "We'll use that on the car and start again to
save for new carpet."

No matter what today has been or what the day may yet
become, it probably won't be without some difficulty. Yet we
can choose how we deal with it.

Will we fret about real as well as anticipated problems?
Will we brood over situations until we create undue stress for
ourselves? Will we allow anxiety to replace sound judgment
necessary for dealing with circumstances?

Jesus addresses worry in plain and simple language: "Who
of you by worrying can add a single hour to his life? Since you
cannot do this very little thing, why do you worry about the
rest?" (Luke 12:25–26).

Sometimes the thin line blurs between useless worry and
sensible concern. But Jesus doesn't *suggest* that we not worry,
he *commands* that we do not worry (Matt. 6:25–34).

What do we worry about? Money? Health? Job? Children? Our weight? Who gets the remote control?

Peter writes a personal invitation to give God all cares and worries: "Humble yourselves, therefore, under God's mighty hand. . . . Cast all your anxiety on him because he cares for you" (1 Pet. 5:6–7).

Worry robs peace of mind and causes unrest. Through his presence, God offers an escape from the heavy fog of worrying. He already knows what's troubling us and probably shakes his head at our delay in turning to him.

Worry and anxiety won't solve problems. Giving them to God is the most effective approach to concerns. God will help us to exchange our worry for his gift of peace of mind.

For great is the LORD *and most worthy of praise.*
(1 Chronicles 16:25)

Keeping in Step

Since we live by the Spirit, let us keep in step with the Spirit.
(Galatians 5:25)

Contemporary society breeds envy; it cultivates our minds
to believe the more things we possess, the happier we will
be. The house, the car, the clothes, and the club membership
become treasured emblems of success.

Our youth today desire what they perceive will improve
their image. They insist on the correct labels on their clothing
and the right kind of car to drive, and frequent only cool places.
They envy and imitate others until they've become alike, trying to be independently different. They see adults grab and
hold tightly to more and more material possessions to secure
their positions in society.

Unchecked greed can cause all manner of hatefulness,
replacing love and respect with conceit and lies. The Bible says
covetousness is an evil thing that starts from within and makes
a person unclean (Mark 7:21–23).

Jesus saw this human problem of greed in his day and
addressed it boldly. Scripture teaches about this problem:
We're not to envy one another (Gal. 5:26), love does not envy
(1 Cor. 13:4), envy will exclude us from heaven (Gal. 5:19–21),
jealously is a powerful force (Prov. 27:4), and "he who hates
covetousness will prolong his days" (Prov. 28:16, NKJV).

Covetousness, envy, jealousy—by whatever name, they
rear their hungry heads through today's materialism. What is
the antidote?

God and his Word. As Christians, we're not to allow envy
in our life. Instead, we can let God's strength consume our
envy. We'll find, as did Paul, if we live our lives for Christ's

sake, in our weakness we will be strong (2 Cor. 12:10). Through his strength we can bear fruits of the Spirit, not those of a sinful nature such as envy, jealousy, and covetousness (Gal. 5:22–26). Then our lifestyles will keep in step with the Holy Spirit.

> *Therefore I will praise you, O LORD, among the nations;*
> *I will sing praise to your name. (2 Samuel 22:50)*

How Many More Towns?

God is our refuge and strength, an ever-present help in trouble.
(Psalm 46:1)

"How many more towns before we get to Granny and Papaw's?" my five-year-old daughter called out from the back seat as we traveled to Tennessee. Each time she asked "How many more towns?" her daddy and I would give an updated number and name familiar towns ahead.

In a Christian's journey toward Heaven we can name some "towns" which lie along the way: difficulty, disappointment, heartache, temptation. But when confronted with these threatening roadblocks, we can take God at his word. We can turn to God for directions.

Life's setbacks may make us wonder how many more will come our way. We need to sharpen our focus on God's sustaining strength to make it through them.

Often we are tempted to be impatient travelers through the life God has planned for us. We ask "How many more towns?" Instead, we can ask God for his help to get through them and on to our destination: eternity with him!

Praise the Lord, for the Lord is good. (Psalm 135:3)

Roses or Thorns?

I have learned to be content whatever the circumstances.
(Philippians 4:11)

When my family complains about the bitter cold of wintry days, I remind them that things could always be worse. Then I point out that when summer comes, they'll wish for these cold days to relieve the sweltering heat. And sure enough, the next August they begin to whine that the days are too hot. When I begin to spout my wisdom, they give me the look, "We know, don't say it. . . . It could be worse."

Do you see the glass of milk half empty rather than half full? Do your friends and family comment that you're often irritable and sulking? Are you unhappy or bored? Do you make yourself and those around you miserable?

When we lapse into our own version of misery, it's up to us how long it stays. At times, we'd welcome an extended leave of absence from life and return when we knew things would be better. Just get away from it all!

The solution isn't that simple. Ignoring discontent usually doesn't remove it. But remaining handcuffed by miseries won't improve the situation either. Bringing about a change requires action that begins within ourselves.

How can we prevent our miseries from taking up permanent residence in our thoughts, our words, and our attitudes?

The apostle Paul says in Romans, "be transformed by the renewing of your mind. Then you will be able to test and approve what God's will is—his good, pleasing and perfect will" (Rom. 12:2).

The word "renew" implies an extensive remaking that results in what was old and soiled becoming like new. Paul urges us to give our mind a make-over, to allow it to come into precise adjustment with the perfect will of God.

Then we can notice the roses more than the thorns; we can see that glass of milk as half full, not half empty. We can regard all aspects of our life in a more positive way.

Ascribe to the Lord the glory due his name. (Psalm 29:2)

2
COMMITMENT

Commitment

When company comes to the house, the responsibility of a cordial get-together usually belongs to the hosts. We put on the coffee pot and set out the cake, making every effort to assure a pleasant time of fellowship with our guests.

Similarly, once we admit the reality of God's presence in our circumstances, preparations by us are necessary in order for a good relationship with him to follow. God has done his part for a right association with us. His side of the formula is complete.

To secure harmonious relations with God, the required action from us is commitment of our life to God's will and purposes.

Yes, we can know God through his son, Jesus, and yes, our eternal destination with him can be certain; but without commitment, our relationship with God will be hobbled, limiting our chance to feel peace even when surrounded by disturbing circumstances.

This desired commitment results when we claim Jesus not only as our Savior but as the ruler of our life. Naming Jesus as our Lord adds a missing ingredient into our relationship with God—an essential ingredient if our relationship is to produce

God-given joy (Phil. 2:11). Holy harmony—this harmonious relation with God—is a natural consequence of surrendering self to God's purposes. This accord prevails when we align our lifestyle with God's perfect guidelines.

Do you experience God's peace in all areas of your life? Fellowship with God helps to smooth the tangles, to straighten the curves, and to level the hills which you face.

Much depends on us to bring about and sustain this tranquility. It's like putting the last puzzle piece into place: God has done his part; he waits for us to do ours. And our part is to give up our stubborn independence and give God his rightful place as Lord of our life (Rom. 10:9). According to Oswald Chambers, "The best measure of spiritual life is not ecstasies but obedience."

Let obedience follow the reality of God's presence in your life. As you read the following pages, may you aim for complete commitment to God and seek his purpose for your life.

How Much Do I Have?

Never be lacking in zeal, but keep your spiritual fervor, serving the Lord. (Romans 12:11)

I stumbled up the hall and stood half asleep at my kitchen sink. Looking through half-closed blinds, I discovered what had interrupted my predawn slumber.

On the deck, several pesky blue jays perched atop the patio table. Aggravated at them for disturbing me, I tapped impatiently on the window. With much fluttering, the birds scattered to nearby trees. All but one.

The lone bird pranced around the table, tilting his head this way and that, beady black eyes searching for his would-be attacker. I raised the mini-blind and tapped fiercely on the glass again. There! He looked my way—he'd found me. He stared at me; I glared at him. Appearing to know my threatening noises couldn't harm him, he didn't budge.

Then the concert began, his music as crisp and crystal clear as the day's spring morning. Each warble imitated his previous one.

Each time he chirped, the little bird quivered from the black collar across his throat to the trembling tip of his brilliant blue tail feathers. Every inch of him moved to produce his melody.

This little bird put all his body behind each note—he gave it all he had. I forgot the blue jay's peskiness, enjoying instead my private recital.

Watching from my quiet kitchen, I thought about his tremendous effort. He certainly didn't go about his singing in a halfhearted way.

Could Christians measure up to the blue jay, I wondered? Are we as committed in our efforts of praise and worship?

I remembered the widow who placed only two coins in the temple treasury as her offering (Mark 12:41–44). Compared to the rich who put in much, the widow's gift pleased Jesus, for he said she "put in everything—all she had to live on" (v. 44).

I recalled when Jesus fed five thousand with only five barley loaves and two fish (John 6:5–14). The bread and fish belonged to a boy in the crowd, apparently all the food he had; but it proved sufficient for Jesus' purpose.

Then I pondered, "How much have I given? How much do I have?"

It makes no difference how much we have. Jesus demands our all when we accept him as our Savior and Lord. Jesus answered the questioning Pharisees, saying the first and greatest commandment is "Love the Lord your God with all your heart and with all your soul and with all your mind" (Matt. 22:37).

All we have. We must give all we have to loving and serving God, whether in our jobs, rearing our children, in our church work, or in our leisure time.

Like the little blue jay on my deck with only one song to sing, we must give it all we've got.

I will praise you, O Lord my God, with all my heart; I will glorify your name forever. (Psalm 86:12)

Rewards of Obedience

"Showing love to a thousand generations of those who love me and keep my commandments." (Exodus 20:6)

C hildren quickly learn the rules of games they wish to play. If they follow them, playtime is generally a happy experience. But if they don't follow the rules, they may suffer a quick consequence: the other children won't permit them to play.

I watched this happen with my children and their friends as they played board games. When one of them attempted to move a game piece a space or two more than allowed, another child extended a restraining hand. Moving a checker piece and changing their mind brought howls of dissent from the opponent. After several tries to bend the rules, the guilty one was pushed out of the group by unanimous consent.

The Ten Commandments are some of God's rules for life. When we dishonor our parents, commit adultery, or lie, unfavorable results occur in our relationships with God and with other people. If we murder and steal, we break not only man's laws but also God's. We can't ignore God and his rules and expect everything to go smoothly. God's instructions are clear: Love me and obey me.

Time and again we read in the Bible of God rewarding obedience. Children and athletes who win their games receive appropriate awards and distinctions. God's reward to those who obey him is continued blessings through his love and care.

Praise the Lord, all you servants of the Lord. (Psalm 134:1)

WHO'S YOUR LEADER?

I am the good shepherd; I know my sheep and my sheep know me. (John 10:14)

"L et's play 'Follow the Leader' and I'm the leader!"
I watched as smiling neighborhood children hurried to line up behind Emily. She had called the game first, appointing herself the leader.

Whatever the game, Emily usually emerged as leader, other children content to comply. They seemed happy to follow her without question.

Peter speaks for the disciples when he tells Jesus, "We have left everything to follow you!" (Matt. 19:27). Levi, the tax collector, obeyed Jesus' command; he "left everything and followed him" (Luke 5:28).

Jesus says, "If anyone would come after me, he must deny himself and take up his cross daily and follow me" (Luke 9:23). When we accept Jesus Christ as Savior we will display this follow-the-leader attitude.

In the parable of the shepherd and his flock (John 10:1–16), Jesus teaches that sheep follow their shepherd "because they know his voice." He says sheep won't follow a stranger; rather they run away because they don't know his voice. Without a shepherd, sheep fall into disarray, scattered about (Mark 14:27).

Jesus is the Good Shepherd. He says, "I know my sheep and my sheep know me" (John 10:14). Christians know Jesus Christ as the genuine shepherd whose direction they follow. A committed Christian won't follow the wrong leader.

He will stand and shepherd his flock in the strength of the LORD, in the majesty of the name of the LORD his God. (Micah 5:4)

Following the Crowd

*Then Saul said to Samuel, "I have sinned. I violated the
Lord's command and your instructions. I was afraid of the
people and so I gave in to them." (1 Samuel 15:24)*

Since the Garden of Eden, humankind continually has tried
to shift blame to another person or another source. Adam
blamed Eve and Eve blamed the serpent. When the consequences of our actions are likely to be bad, we attempt to
shrug off our responsibility.

Saul tried to justify his disobedience by saying he had listened to the people because he feared them (1 Sam. 15:24–31).
Whether acting alone or from listening to the people, Saul had
failed to obey God. Consequently, God rejected Saul as king.

From the time we're first able to reason, our peers exert
influence on our decision-making processes. However, through
God's strength we can control how much destructive peer influence we allow into our lives.

Our youth have new options today, including numerous
anti-drug efforts such as the Drug Abuse Resistance Education
(D.A.R.E.) program. Through D.A.R.E. youngsters are instructed
in eight ways to say no to drugs instead of being led into their
abuse. The "True Love Waits" project urges teenagers and young
adults to make a public commitment to enter marriage sexual-
ly pure. The Promise Keepers movement offers an arena for
men to turn away from being the world's kind of man and
commit themselves to a life pleasing to Jesus Christ.

Availing ourselves of these and similar programs encourages
us to flee evil temptations and instead follow righteousness
with those who also call on the Lord (2 Tim. 2:22). We can be
vigilant in our associations knowing that "bad company cor-
rupts good character" (1 Cor. 15:33).

We don't have to be pressured by the crowd as Saul claimed to have been. Then we won't need to cast blame on others for our actions. Instead, we can sift all peer pressures through a filter of God's instruction with the determination that we will obey him.

> *May all the kings of the earth praise you, O LORD, when they hear the words of your mouth. (Psalm 138:4)*

Public Intentions

The people all responded together, "We will do everything the Lord *has said." (Exodus 19:8)*

People who try to break a bad habit usually receive the same piece of advice: Make it known to someone else. Whether it's losing weight, stopping smoking, or spending less money, it probably will go better if we share our vow of self-improvement.

That way it will be easier not to give up when temptation becomes strong. When we almost take that second helping or make that foolish purchase on credit, someone will be able to encourage us to withstand our destructive temptations. We'll stick closer to our convictions because others know about them. This principle underlies many successful recovery programs.

This element of accountability holds true in our efforts toward a mature Christian walk. Sharing our love and obedience to God with other believers will gain their support of our desires to become more like Jesus. When we proclaim our convictions publicly among other Christians, we strengthen our vows to God. We can then go about his work with encouragement from those who also align themselves with the Lord.

They will speak of the glorious splendor of your majesty, and I will meditate on your wonderful works. (Psalm 145:5)

WHEN THE LOAD'S TOO HEAVY

Blessed is he whose help is the God of Jacob, whose hope is in the LORD his God. (Psalm 146:5)

The Israelites were in the second year of their journey from Egypt to the Promised Land (Num. 11). Tired of the manna God had provided since their second month of travel, they again questioned their decision to follow Moses. They whined, "If only we had meat to eat!" (Num. 11:4).

Doing what God had called him to do, leading these ungrateful people through the wilderness, tried Moses' patience. Feeling inadequate, Moses spat out a string of questions at God. Moses seems to have said, "What did I do to deserve this? I'm trying to do what you told me to do."

Finally, Moses declared the burden too heavy. His despair reached such low depths that he offered to die rather than continue under the weight of his responsibilities. God not only gave Moses help with his burdens, but also dealt with the cause of his hopelessness.

What causes you despair? Impossible burdens and responsibilities like Moses? Great disappointments? Rejections?

When we are faithful, God proves his power over our despair as he did for Moses. Through prayer we can ask for God's help with our burdens. For his obedient servants, God is their God of hope.

But as for me, I will always have hope; I will praise you more and more. (Psalm 71:14)

A Better Way

Commit your way to the Lord; trust in him. (Psalm 37:5)

Almost every time I visit a nearby large city, I notice major changes in the interstate highway system. Road construction always makes driving more difficult.

A friend who lives in the city gives me tips about which way to go to avoid problem areas. Sometimes he advises me to take the bypass loop to stay away from downtown congestion. Other times I'm told the interstate route through the heart of the city will be a better choice. Without some advance warning from my friend, I would be a helpless victim of the detours and backed-up traffic at construction sites.

Through his Word, God gives us a chance to know ahead of time where trouble may lie on our roadways of life. He doesn't want us to run headlong into detours that might obscure our witness or lead us away from the faith.

God tells us these things so that we may find a better way. Usually this means taking stock of our present goals and priorities, holding them up to his standards. Then we can make adjustments that keep us in the best lane.

I will praise the Lord, who counsels me. (Psalm 16:7)

Giving Yourself

They gave themselves first to the Lord and then to us in keeping with God's will. (2 Corinthians 8:5)

T hroughout my childhood, and even today when I'm sick, my mother says, "I'd take every bit of your pain on myself if I could. I would gladly take your place." How willingly parents give of themselves in order to help their children!

Our role model for such sacrificial and spontaneous giving is God. He gave himself unselfishly for us through his Son. God voluntarily gave Jesus to the world in exchange for all our sins. Jesus carried our sin burden to the cross where he suffered our physical pain. Through Jesus' crucifixion, God took our place; he gave himself for us.

The Macedonians had their priorities in the correct order. Only after they gave themselves to God did they give to Paul's collection for needy believers (2 Cor. 8:1–5). Having given themselves, through God's grace they could then give their resources according to his will.

Giving ourselves to God is like pouring milk from a pitcher. When we empty out all worldly cares, we make a dwelling place for God. He bathes us with his love until we feel as refreshed as the earth after a spring rain. This complete surrender to God allows his will to work in our lives. A radiance begins from within and whatever else we do is done joyfully within his will.

Through Jesus, therefore, let us continually offer to God a sacrifice of praise—the fruit of lips that confess his name. (Hebrews 13:15)

CALL WAITING

"Take my yoke upon you and learn from me." (Matthew 11:29)

I wonder if Alexander Graham Bell ever envisioned electronic beepers and telephones which signal when someone is trying to call us while we're already talking. Could Mr. Bell possibly have imagined the future of communication? Wireless transmission, cellular phones, laptop computers—undoubtedly it would please him that long distance contact with another is possible even in the deepest jungle or on vast deserts.

But none of these electronic gadgets are useful unless we plug into them properly. We may see a message for us on the computer screen or hear the beeper at our waist plead for our attention. The call waiting signal may cut in on our telephone conversation. But we don't have to answer any of these interruptions. We may choose to ignore these attempts to communicate with us.

And even if we do venture into a conversation, we may break the connection at any time and turn our attention to something else. Whatever claims highest priority with us will keep us the longest.

Can you imagine God trying to get through to you? Because of other interests that claim your time, he finds your line is frequently busy. Or you won't answer your beep or heed the call waiting signal.

And sometimes when he does have your attention, perhaps even in prayer, your mind wanders off to something you find more interesting. Our world makes it easy to turn God on and off, to put him in a box and take him out when we need him.

In whatever fashion God's beep comes, it's his way of getting in touch with us. We can answer his call or continue doing what we're more interested in at the time. We can tune him in or tune him out.

God's call is always waiting for us to complete the connection, to stay plugged in to his voice, to align ourselves with God's plan for us and receive his message, to give him undivided attention.

My mouth will speak in praise of the LORD. Let every creature praise his holy name for ever and ever. (Psalm 145:21)

It's Up to Us

But Noah found favor in the eyes of the LORD. (Genesis 6:8)

M y young son understood about the safety of wearing his seat belt when riding in a car, but all his urgings couldn't convince his grandmother to buckle up. Frustrated, he'd say, "Granny, if you want to die, then don't buckle up—it's up to you!"

Back in Genesis, God probably felt similar frustration toward the human race because of their extreme wickedness. The sons of God, thought to have been leaders in Seth's bloodline, intermarried with godless descendants of Cain. These abnormal marriages which God didn't want filled the land with corruption and violence. Despite having every chance to live by God's commands, humans chose to gratify the desires of their sinful natures. God saw that man's every thought was evil all day. Finally, his period of urging was over.

Grieved that he had made man, God decided to destroy his creation by floodwaters. Even so, hope remained because Noah's godly living pleased God. Through this righteous man, God gave humankind another chance for survival (Gen. 6:1–8).

Just as my son couldn't make his grandmother wear her seat belt, God won't force us to live a life pleasing to him. But if we choose godly living, we'll learn the wisdom of obeying God. We will survive the deluge of wickedness in our world, just as Noah did in his. It's up to us.

I will praise you forever for what you have done; in your name I will hope, for your name is good. (Psalm 52:9)

3

PROVISION

Provision

GOD'S HELP FOR COPING WITH MORTAL NEEDS

[God takes care] of those who love him and keep his commands (Deut. 7:9).

Jesus tells about a son who asked his father for bread (Matt. 7:9–11). The story explains that no caring parent would substitute a stone for the bread. In the same way, no parent would endanger his offspring by offering him a serpent instead of a fish to eat.

Jesus' lesson in this parable is clear and understandable. He compares the reaction of an earthly father with that of our heavenly Father. The superiority of God's provision is undeniable—"*how much more* will your Father in heaven give good gifts to those who ask him!" (v. 11, italics mine). "How much more" speaks of the abundance of God's provision.

God will fulfill our needs. Not our wants, but he's available for any measure of provision toward our needs. God supplies divine strength to battle mortal needs and, in fact, will wage our battles for us (2 Chron. 20:15).

"God is our refuge and strength, an ever-present help in trouble" (Ps. 46:1). That's a promise from God's Word. A promise he regularly honors for me when I nurse sick children, grieve the death of a loved one, or face exhausting work. Whatever my need, God sustains me.

Often I'm like a child who can't swim but who insists on going to the deep end of the pool. I follow Satan into situations where I'm unable to survive unless God reaches out to help me. Like a watchful lifeguard, God pulls me back to safety. Even though God's Word posts his rules beside the swimming pool of life, I sometimes ignore them and need rescuing.

Even more than a dedicated earthly parent, God wants to give me strength to resist Satan's temptations. Strength when I am too weak to fight my battles alone. Jesus says, "My grace is sufficient for you, for my power is made perfect in weakness" (2 Cor. 12:9–10).

How much more! With the proper perspective and total commitment we can experience "how much more." As you continue to read, I hope the following pages will help you discover the abundance of God's provision.

Catch Me!

Trust in the LORD forever, for the LORD, the LORD, is the Rock eternal (Isaiah 26:4)

One sunny, spring afternoon, my three-year-old grand-daughter, Mallory, asked me to push her in the swing. Soon tiring of that activity, she hopped off and scampered up the ladder to the slide. In an instant, Mallory discovered that she had a problem: the metal was too hot from the sunshine for her to rest her bare legs against so she could slide down.

Compounding her dilemma, Mallory couldn't climb back down the ladder.

I walked toward the slide, thinking that she would ask me to lift her off. But, without warning, Mallory leapt through the air toward me. In quick reflex I wrapped my arms around her just as she latched on to me.

Mallory had chosen me as an escape from her perch atop the slide—she hadn't once thought that I wouldn't be strong enough to catch her.

"You catched me!" Mallory shouted, laughing and taking my face in her hands, rewarding me with a kiss. "Momma Jo, I love you," she said, again tightening her arms around my neck.

Mallory's leap of faith reminds me of the simplicity of Jesus' teaching. In his Word, he promises to be with me at my exact moment of need. I am assured that if I accept God's promises with the innocence and the trust of a little child, I can know his peace (Phil. 4:7).

Be exalted, O LORD, in your strength; we will sing and praise your might. (Psalm 21:13)

Expert Available

Cast your cares on the Lord and he will sustain you.
(Psalm 55:22)

A business associate related to me how she could claim sleep the moment her eyes closed. Then a neighbor filed a lawsuit against her. The neighbor fell at my friend's home, causing permanent disabilities. My friend's insurance agent assured her she had adequate coverage and had nothing to worry about. But, convincing herself that she faced a real possibility of losing every material possession, my friend began experiencing sleepless nights, something alien to her until now.

After a few fretful weeks of trying to deal with the problem, she retained a law firm to represent her. Relieved that someone more qualified now had control of her legal problems, she went home and slept through the night!

This same principle paves the way toward relief for Christians when we retain Jesus Christ to represent us.

When we try to be self-sufficient in the face of distress, many times we tend to get bogged down deeper. Our problem doesn't get solved, but increases. Facing our frustrations, we conclude we need an expert to bail us out, someone more qualified to deal with our particular concern.

That's when we should share our burden with God. We can allow him to lessen our worrisome load because he is the expert we need. He can take charge.

We can experience tremendous relief by surrendering our burdens to God. The problem may not immediately go away and may never completely be solved. But knowing that we have someone to help, that we don't have to carry the responsibility all alone, we gain victory over sleepless nights and fretful days.

God invites us to share our oppressive burdens with him, promising to deliver us from them.

His request of us in return for his help is to honor him (Ps. 50:15). Honor him! What a simple gesture on our part. Then we can rest our head on the pillow at bedtime, knowing we've released our day's problems into God's competent hands!

O LORD, you are my God; I will exalt you and praise your name, for in perfect faithfulness you have done marvelous things. (Isaiah 25:1)

WHAT A DEAL!

"'I carried you on eagles' wings and brought you to myself.'"
(Exodus 19:4)

T he strength of an eagle is well known. But when young eagles first leave their nests, they cannot fly well. Their untried wings flap awkwardly in their attempts to soar across the sky. The mother eagle glides nearby, waiting until the eaglet's tired wings no longer support it. She then flies beneath her struggling youngster and spreads long, broad wings to catch it. The strong, stiff feathers in her wings hold the weight of the eaglet.

Through his grace and mercy, God provides similar security for his people. He will undergird us, carrying us through our trials and temptations.

A few days after moving to a new city, my husband's work took him out of town overnight. I ran my necessary errands and returned home with my small child well before dark. I closed the curtains and checked all the locks. Still my anxieties and fears ran high. I heard every creak of the new house as I settled in for the night; I prayed for God's watchful care and slept.

In the morning, I couldn't find my keys to drive my daughter to school. Finally, we found them where they had been all night: hanging in the back door lock—on the outside! What security God granted us through the night! More than I even knew to ask for.

God supports us in times of need. He wants to gather us close for fellowship with him.

In return, he desires our love and obedience. What a small price to pay for the unlimited grace of God. What a deal!

Splendor and majesty are before him; strength and glory are in his sanctuary. (Psalm 96:6)

Unseen Protection

For the Angel of the LORD guards and rescues all who reverence him. (Psalm 34:7 TLB)

For many years, I've prayed daily for God to place his angels around my children throughout their nights and days. I've entreated God for this angel-presence to protect my children, particularly as they grew up and out of my physical reach.

One summer, my daughter and her four-year-old twins went outside to water flowers in their front yard. The children stood a few feet from the porch steps.

After turning on the water faucet, my daughter, Paige, pulled the attached water hose toward some pink and red impatiens across the yard. About half way to the black pot of flowers, the hose balked at her tugging, refusing to yield another inch. Before Paige could straighten the tangled hose, her son screamed, "A snake! A snake!" Alan jumped up and down.

Even though her knees almost buckled with fright, Paige scooted Alan and his sister Mallory up the steps toward the front door, all the while yelling for her husband. Jeff rushed from the backyard, seeing the snake at once. Paige and the children watched from the safety of the house as Jeff killed the snake and removed it from the yard.

Later, Jeff went to unscramble the water hose and finish watering the impatiens. He found the hose lying neatly coiled, ready to move freely in any direction it might be pulled.

Paige had to inspect the hose for herself, its resistance had been so strong. She and Jeff calculated that if she had moved with the water hose only a few more steps, her feet would have intersected the snake's path.

When hearing about this, I had no doubts that an angel held back the water hose to prevent my daughter moving closer to the snake and into harm's way.

I've often wondered if I bother God with my constant requests of angel protection for my children. I'm thankful he relented to my persistent prayers like the judge gave in to the widow in Luke 18.

I'll continue to pray for angels to watch over my family wherever they may go.

I call to the LORD, who is worthy of praise, and I am saved from my enemies. (2 Samuel 22:4)

Mountain Guide

By day the Lord *went ahead of them in a pillar of cloud to guide them on their way and by night in a pillar of fire to give them light, so that they could travel by day or night. (Ex. 13:21)*

M y cousin, Muriel, and her daughter Sandi were driving home to Tennessee after spending Thanksgiving with relatives in Detroit. As they neared the Cumberland Mountains, they hit a blinding snowstorm. The radio warned of treacherous conditions. Phone lines were down. Theirs was the lone car approaching the foothills.

Straightening in the driver's seat, Sandi gripped the steering wheel tightly. "Dad's expecting us," she said.

Muriel was anxious to get back, too. "Okay," she agreed, "let's keep going."

They started uphill. They both strained to see the signs marking the winding road, but the windshield wipers were no match for the driving snow. "I can't see," Sandi said.

They'd made a terrible decision. They couldn't turn around. "God, please guide us," they prayed aloud.

"Look!" Muriel shouted. A light glowed hazily in the distance, fifty feet ahead. "Follow that vehicle!" Snow covered the road signs now, but the light moved on steadily, like a beacon.

An hour passed, and they began their descent. Through every bend and dip in the road, the distance between them and the light remained constant until finally they rounded the last curve. They looked ahead. No other vehicle was on the road.

They wanted to thank their guide. "He's got to be in here," Sandi said, pulling into a diner.

When they walked in, the customers stared. "How did you get over that mountain?" the waitress asked. "No one has come across in hours."

The all-powerful light had guided them.

"O Lord, the great and awesome God." (Daniel 9:4)

Choosing to Forget

"I will forgive their wickedness and will remember their sins no more." (Hebrews 8:12)

Scrapbooks usually contain no tokens of bad memories; we save only good mementos. In a thick book with sturdy blank pages, we collect a lifetime of pleasant keepsakes. Later, we'll drag out the old red scrapbook and pressed gardenia corsages fill our nostrils with their remembered sweetness. The book bulges with the junior-senior banquet program, newspaper clippings about the DAR award and basketball games, and photos from the Beta Club convention. We delightfully relive our good times through its pages.

Sometimes, however, when we mentally review our life, we dwell on regret and self-reproach. In our mind we've filled volumes with past sins. Beyond yellowing photos and newspaper clippings in a tattered scrapbook, our mind's eye recalls the ugly grievances we try in vain to forget: teenage rebellion against God's laws when we thought they kept us from having fun; disobedience as a young adult when we spent all those heady paychecks selfishly, not giving back to God; the bargaining we slung in God's face when we promised him we'd go to church every Sunday if he would just make a way to purchase that new car.

We try to forget our lack of praise to God for giving us his Son to save us; our meager thanksgiving for his care through illness; our faltering faithfulness toward him when we ignore his instruction to feed his sheep.

If we have repented and been forgiven for these and other sins, we create our own guilt when we choose to remember them.

God says that when he forgives us for sinning, he also forgets our sin (Heb. 8:12; 10:17). He separates us from our sin as far as the east is from the west (Ps. 103:12). Why can't we be as kind toward ourselves?

We build scrapbooks like God treats sin: we keep only good memories. With God's help we can live in the same manner. We can release our forgiven sins and forget them. God has.

I will praise you, O LORD, with all my heart; I will tell of all your wonders. (Psalm 9:1)

Answering the Knock

Let us hold firmly to the faith we profess. (Hebrews 4:14)

T he night before Daddy's funeral, grief and devastation crushed me. His untimely death couldn't be in accord with the will of a caring God! The Bible teaches that God wants his followers to be blessed. Well, I was forty years old and I had lost my daddy; I didn't feel blessed.

Well-meaning friends and family members offered words of encouragement. "Your father is out of his pain," one said. "God works everything out for the best," another explained.

Nobody's words helped. I could find no answers.

That night while everyone else slept, I stared into the thick darkness. I lay awake in my girlhood bed, smothering sobs into the pillow. The old dresser mirror usually reflected light from the window and sprayed it across the room. But not tonight. The cloudy night sky had shut out any moonlight, eliminating any rescue from the stifling darkness. The loud silence fell around me like a net.

How could I pray *tonight*? How could I pray to God when he had taken my daddy from me?

But I did pray. In the beginning I lashed out. I poured out my feelings of anger, hurt, and doubt. God listened as these emotions drained from me.

Frustrations released, my conversation with God then took on a calmness and I lay still. I didn't know the proper words to use to ask God for healing of my heartache. But God already knew about my need. He waited patiently until I was ready to receive the strength he offered.

Suddenly I sensed God's nearness washing over me. The closed bedroom door had been no barrier to him. I felt God's presence enter the room.

Without looking, I somehow was aware he stood quietly at the foot of the bed. Fear kept my face turned away from him. A mixture of fear and reverence.

I wasn't afraid of what I would discover him to be; I feared the impression he would have of me. After all, I'd just lashed out at him from my prison of pain! What would he think of me?

He waited for me to respond to the reality of his presence. Finally, resting on an elbow, I looked over my shoulder into a blinding, but serene, light. I knew without doubt there was life in that bright and steady radiance. Fingers of white light brighter than the sun reached toward me. I felt a gentle transfusion of incredible peace, almost as if I were at once one with the light. It touched the deepest part of me.

Braver, I sat upright in bed and looked full into the light, certain I was in God's presence. I heard no words, but all at once I felt my tensions evaporate. I could feel loving arms of comfort wrap around me, holding me close. Without any hesitation, I surrendered to the light's caress and my body relaxed as soothing sleep captured me.

The next morning I felt refreshed. My anger at God from the night before was now replaced with a feeling of assurance. God *had* visited me in that blessed light. His tranquil strength *would* cushion me against the afternoon when I must give Daddy my last earthly good-bye.

I'll never forget the appearance of that white light, recalling it countless times since then. I'm as certain today as I was that night in my dark bedroom that God came to me in that light. He came to me during my need, offering all the help I would accept.

The transformation I experienced in the presence of that light remains with me. God came closer to me when I needed him and that has made all the difference in the world in my priorities. My focus and faith in God since have been stronger than I'd ever thought possible.

The presence of God revealed to me years ago testifies to the reality of the Scripture, "Here I am! I stand at the door and knock. If anyone hears my voice and opens the door, I will come in" (Rev. 3:20).

In your darkest hour, allow God to come close. Think more on God than on your discouragement and invite him into your life. He's waiting just outside your heart's door.

I will praise the LORD all my life; I will sing praise to my God as long as I live. (Psalm 146:2)

Bread of Life

Then Jesus declared, "I am the bread of life. He who comes to me will never go hungry, and he who believes in me will never be thirsty." (John 6:35)

A local ministry to drug abusers offers wholesome meals and a place to stay. Adults entering the shelter know its reputation: At some point they will hear the gospel message.

To satisfy their need for food and lodging, they're willing to subject themselves to "Jesus people" who operate the shelter.

The day after Jesus fed the multitudes with the five loaves and two fish (John 6:5–13), the people searched him out again. Jesus told the crowd that he knew they sought him, not because of his miraculous signs, but because they wanted more food from him (John 6:26).

Then on this day, with that background, he seized the opportunity to discuss a need greater than a physical need. He offered them "bread" unlike any they had ever known.

Jesus challenges his followers to spread the Good News of salvation (Mark 16:15). In our attempts to tell others about Jesus' saving grace we may encounter people with physical needs. Our task then will be to feed and clothe them. Doing so will encourage them to become more receptive to any teaching we may do. That's the way Jesus reached people on this and other occasions. Do we need a better example? Our ministry is not complete until we introduce them to Jesus, the Bread of Life.

Then will I ever sing praise to your name. (Psalm 61:8)

A Way Out

But when you are tempted, he will also provide a way out so that you can stand up under it. (1 Corinthians 10:13)

Temptation was the magnet which lured humankind into the original sin in the Garden of Eden. Satan's enticements achieved the seduction of Adam and Eve.

Do Satan's tricks snare us into his web of sin? Do we, like the apostle Paul, have good intentions only to fail (Rom. 7:18–20)?

Some would mislead us by saying that temptation comes from God. But know for sure that God does not tempt anyone (James 1:13). The tempter is Satan. Satan was bold enough to tempt even Jesus (Matt. 4:3–11; Mark 1:13). Why would he hesitate to tempt us?

We don't have to confront our temptations from a powerless position. God's grace helps us to say no (Titus 2:11–12).

The Bible offers the formula for resisting temptation. First, we're to live within the direction of the Holy Spirit, and we "will not gratify the desires of the sinful nature" (Gal. 5:16). Secondly, Jesus advises his disciples to "pray that you will not fall into temptation" (Luke 22:40). He tells them "the spirit is willing but the body is weak" (Matt. 26:41). Just what Paul explained—the weak, sinful nature.

Finally, we're encouraged to protect ourselves against Satan's schemes by putting on the armor of God: truth, righteousness, faith, salvation, the Word of God, and prayer (Eph. 6:10–18).

Jesus can sympathize with us in our weakness against temptation because he was tempted in all points as we are (Heb. 4:15). But, you may ask, did Jesus meet temptation from a possible affair with a co-worker or neighbor? From the opportunity to get that promotion with a little deception or to improve his mood by simply turning to drugs?

It's true, Jesus never stood in our exact position of temptation. But he faced situations which breed the same feelings we experience—the *pain* of the cross, the *loneliness* and *depression* of the Garden of Gethsemane.

Scripture promises that (1) God will not allow us to be tempted beyond what we can bear, and (2) will provide us a way out so we can endure the temptation (1 Cor. 10:13).

It's difficult to take advice from someone who hasn't walked in our shoes. If they haven't been there, we think, they just can't know how we feel. How could they help us?

But God has been there. Remember, Satan tempted Jesus just as Satan tempts us daily. But God can provide an escape from Satan's traps: "Come near to God and he will come near to you" (James 4:8). God's majestic nearness leaves less room for Satan's presence.

Great is the LORD and most worthy of praise; his greatness no one can fathom. (Psalm 145:3)

Equipment for Valley Travel

"Do not let your hearts be troubled. Trust in God; trust also in me." (John 14:1)

My bedside vigil stretched into days as I watched meningitis suck precious life from the still form of my college-age daughter. Three times this week, we'd rushed her to the emergency room, received treatment, and been sent home, only to repeat the cycle a few hours later. Finally, when no medication stopped her body's swelling, the doctor admitted her to the hospital.

Sunday afternoon, I sat alone with Paige, watching the disease apparently winning its battle. Gone was the twinkle in her eyes and the ready smile on her lips. The nurse had just left, the same one who had been coming in every fifteen minutes to take vital signs. Pained and discouraged, I watched as she recorded a blood pressure reading only half what it should be.

Alone again in the hospital room, each of us experienced our own unique agony. Lying curled in a fetal position, my daughter moved only her eyes. With them almost swollen shut, she looked up at me through her consuming torture.

"Mother, this may be my time to die," she whispered. No panic or fear registered in her words or in her fevered eyes.

This same thought had been silently hammering inside my mind all afternoon. Holding her limp hand in mine, I leaned down closer and said quietly, "Darling, it may be." She shared a labored smile with me and slowly closed her eyes.

Amazingly, I didn't curse God or offer him any arguments or attempt to bargain with him to spare her life. I knew without doubt Paige believed in God's Son and trusted him for her salvation and eternal life.

As precious minutes slipped away in that lonely hospital room, I recalled Jesus' words as fresh as if he spoke them for the first time that day: "Do not let your hearts be troubled. Trust in God; trust also in me" (John 14:1). Then Jesus promised, "Peace I leave with you; my peace I give you. I do not give to you as the world gives. Do not let your hearts be troubled and do not be afraid" (John 14:27). I believed if God chose to take my daughter that day, he would in turn supply me with "the peace of God, which transcends all understanding" (Phil. 4:7).

I trusted God for his comfort and everlasting strength to support me (Isa. 26:4). I rested in the assurance that Paige claimed these same promises. Peace covered her swollen face as she closed her eyes. We both accepted God's will.

After evening church services that day, our pastor and his wife came by. They barely concealed their shock at seeing Paige's hands and face twice their normal size. After encouraging her, they prayed with us in that still quiet hospital room.

Looking back, I can only believe that God influenced every move Paige's doctors and nurses made. On Monday, her health changed unbelievably for the better. By Wednesday morning she was fully recovered. The doctors released her from their care.

Later that day our pastor found Paige's hospital bed empty. He asked about her at the nurses' station. Later he told us how much the nurses had marveled about her unexplainable recovery. "It's just a miracle that she survived," one nurse told him. We all smile now, knowing what absolute truth she spoke.

Does a Christian experience valleys between the mountaintop experiences? Yes. The trying days when it seemed I might outlive my daughter were the deepest valleys I've traveled.

God promises his buffering strength and calming peace for valley travel. We can always cling to his promises, "For he himself is our peace" (Eph. 2:14).

Now, our God, we give you thanks, and praise your glorious name. (1 Chronicles 29:13)

4

SECURITY

Security

Today the market for security systems flourishes. Homes, offices, and automobiles are guarded by electronic mechanisms which blare, alerting anyone within earshot. Additionally, many buildings are connected to the local police who respond quickly in an emergency.

We live in a time when many people carry guns and build high fences. They leave nothing to chance when considering security.

God left nothing to chance in the area of his children's security. He sent his son, Jesus Christ, to earth with a message about eternal safety. He offered a complete protection system for those who would believe and call on the name of Jesus (John 3:16).

God promises that when we accept Jesus as Lord, he will grant us eternal life (Rom. 10:13). He invites our belief in Jesus as our Savior. Because of his promises and our belief, we may know for sure that we have this eternal life.

God arranged for the eternal security of each of us when he sacrificed Jesus Christ for us and our sinful nature. Once we claim Jesus, we remain his forever (Rom. 8:38–39), shielded by his loving protection.

No wonder Jesus identifies himself as the Good Shepherd (John 10:11)—the one who safeguards his flock. What a promise of protection!

May you learn from the following selections that you can expect and receive God's salvation and care. May you develop complete confidence in God's constant reliability. "Because of the LORD's great love we are not consumed, for his compassions never fail. They are new every morning; great is your faithfulness" (Lam. 3:22–23).

LOST AND FOUND

"There is rejoicing . . . over one sinner who repents."
(Luke 15:10)

While shopping, I overheard a mother comforting her small child.

"Let's go to the Lost and Found office," she said. "We'll ask the man if he's found your doll."

"But, Mother," the child said, "how could the man find my doll? He doesn't even know it's lost."

Jesus teaches about losing something, then actively searching to find it: a man who had one hundred sheep, but lost one (Matt. 18:10–14); a woman who lost one of ten silver coins (Luke 15:8–10). In these biblical accounts, great happiness occurs when diligent searching finds the lost sheep and the lost coin.

Ending the parable of the lost coin, Jesus says, "In the same way, I tell you, there is rejoicing in the presence of the angels of God over one sinner who repents" (Luke 15:10). But repentance occurs only after a sinner realizes his lost condition.

Sinners must actively seek redemption through Jesus Christ's sacrificial blood (Eph. 1:7). Through God's grace, Jesus can pluck them from their sins' darkness. He will forgive those sins, making a person fit for the kingdom of God (Col. 1:13–14). But a sinner must first seek salvation before he can find it.

Have you been lost . . . and found? If not, repent—be sorry for your sins. Ask God to forgive you for them. Accept his Son Jesus as Lord in your life. Rejoicing will occur when you are no longer lost but are found.

Heal me, O LORD, and I will be healed; save me and I will be saved, for you are the one I praise. (Jeremiah 17:14)

SHELTER FROM THE STORMS

"I would hurry to my place of shelter, far from the tempest and storm." (Psalm 55:8)

O ur eleven-year-old English shepherd dog, Lady, hides from thunderstorms. Hearing the first faint rumble, Lady tucks her bushy tail, creeps toward her doghouse, and crawls inside. She remains there until skies clear.

Watching Lady's behavior, I'm reminded how we can turn toward God at trouble's first nudge. Lady's doghouse gives her shelter from the storm; God can do the same for us. He offers us shelter from life's turbulence. Just as an earthly father provides for his children, God can give us much more (Matt. 7:9–11).

During periods of work outside the home, I encountered co-workers who enjoyed swapping off-color jokes. I felt that if I listened willingly, I compromised my Christian principles. So I said no and walked away. On these occasions I ran toward God's protection against temptation that weakens my faith.

Satan prowls around looking for those he can destroy (1 Pet. 5:8). When we sense his threats to our Christian commitment, we can follow Lady's example: Move away from impending danger; hurry to our Shelter.

I call to the LORD, who is worthy of praise, and I am saved from my enemies. (Psalm 18:3)

The Great Mediator

The people remained at a distance, while Moses approached the thick darkness where God was. (Exodus 20:21)

I was once secretary to a department head who supervised thirty engineers. To help him use his time wisely, my boss appointed me to be his mediator.

I'd collect problems and complaints from the engineers and then compile them on a summary sheet for the boss. He dealt with many of the items himself. The rest he answered back through me. Since I knew both sides of the discussions, this process made handling daily tasks more efficient and proved satisfactory for all.

God used Moses as his mediator to communicate with the Israelites. Today we have a new mediator. God gave his Son, Jesus, as the one through whom we may approach him (1 Tim. 2:5).

Rarely can someone in my position walk into the office of a large company's CEO. If I knew someone who knew someone who knew the CEO, I might get my foot in the door. Very often it really is a matter of who you know.

Whenever I want to approach God, I mention the name of Jesus. Using the name of Jesus is the only way to approach his throne and have unhindered contact with the Father. This is really a miracle—*we* have total access to a holy God.

Scripture assures us we will be heard by God through his Son, who offers our praise and petitions to God.

Let the name of the LORD be praised both now and forevermore. (Psalm 113:2)

No Invitation Required

The Spirit helps us in our weakness. (Romans 8:26)

Reality settled in when my parents' car drove out of sight. I was finally "in college," but words couldn't describe how lonely I felt in the first moments after my parents' farewell. My assigned roommate hadn't arrived. I had met no one. I was alone.

Loneliness draped heavy across my shoulders. I felt isolated despite the bustle of other people moving around me. A painful longing choked off my ability to move. I wanted to run after the car and wrap myself in the comfort of the two people inside.

In spite of these consuming feelings, I wanted to burst victoriously onto this new scene and belong. To combat being lonely, it's easy to depend on peers and surroundings for help. Peer acceptance seems to fill most voids at any age. But gaining that acceptance sometimes requires that we step knee-deep into peer-pressure quagmire. That decision can suck us into a position where we're never alone, yet still lonely.

Society presents attractive cures for loneliness. We only have to watch television commercials. They show us beautiful people flooded with pleasure, seemingly with no responsibility. The not-so-subtle messages lure us into the false belief that life could really be that much fun, that attractive, *all the time*, for everybody.

When loneliness doesn't wait for an invitation and sometimes overstays its welcome, God's support provides comfort. We don't have to depend on exaggerated beauty of worldly pleasures and acceptance.

God gives his Holy Spirit to help and comfort us in our weaknesses—even in loneliness (Rom. 8:26). You don't have to feel weak and alone. God sent the Holy Spirit as one you can turn to. God lives within you by the Spirit. Even when you don't know what to pray for, he intercedes with the Father on your behalf (Rom. 8:26–27).

The Holy Spirit did his job for me that crisp, fall day I started college. He gave my legs the will to move, protected me, and supplied me with the right words to say. Today you can ask God to give you the Holy Spirit to dwell within you and strengthen you (Luke 11:13).

The heavens praise your wonders, O LORD, your faithfulness too, in the assembly of the holy ones. (Psalm 89:5)

TIE A KNOT AND HANG ON!

"I will give you rest." (Matthew 11:28)

Which of these statements describe you or your situation?

1. There's not enough time in the day to get everything done.
2. Loving concern motivates my daily visits to an elderly family member, but still my body bears the tiring effects.
3. I just can't find the strength to battle the rebellious spirit of my teenager.
4. The car always breaks down the same day I must go out of town, go to the doctor's office, go to the grocery store . . .
5. I don't resent the sleepless near-dawn hours walking the floor with my newborn, but nevertheless I reap exhausted daylight hours.
6. When I finally reach "Go," someone hands me a card that says go back ten spaces.
7. All of the above.
8. Some of the above plus at least a dozen more.

At week's end, our energy reserves depleted, we're just plain worn out! We even begin to wonder if we'll ever be our old self again, alert and eager for any challenge. We're so overcome with obligations and commitments!

The new day never seems as refreshing anymore; unfinished yesterdays spill over their boundaries, causing today rarely to begin on its own just-washed chalkboard. We wonder how we can look forward to another day like all those before it.

Experience convinces us that we'll only stand in a downpour of never-ending fatigue. We know we'll be unable to stay ahead of the avalanche of responsibilities.

Sound familiar?

Growing weary in life is universal. Humankind, so often tired and discouraged, would benefit from the instruction in Hebrews 3:13 to encourage one another daily.

Self encouragement comes from thinking on Jesus' earthly existence. When I'm sure I can't meet another need for my family or friends, I remind myself of Jesus' suffering and humiliation on his heavy cross. By this comparison, my tiring tasks measure less significant. Looking to Jesus and recalling the hostility he endured, I gain his strength to pick me up out of my blinding weariness and discouragement (Heb. 12:3).

A persevering faith in God outweighs weariness. Jesus extends his personal invitation, "Come to me, all you who are weary and burdened, and I will give you rest" (Matt. 11:28).

Helping to prepare us for life after graduation, my high school principal offered some sound advice to our senior class. "When the going gets tough," he said, "and life is slipping too quickly through your fingers, tie a knot and hang on!" I would add, have faith that God won't let the knot unravel!

So, with courageous faith in God, we won't lose heart, won't get discouraged. We can tie our knot securely with God's love. God promises rest for those who believe and patiently depend on him (Heb. 4:3,9; Matt. 11:28).

Praise the LORD, O my soul. O LORD my God, you are very great; you are clothed with splendor and majesty. (Psalm 104:1)

Who Is God's Equal?

The LORD is the everlasting God. . . . He will not grow tired or weary. (Isaiah 40:28)

The first time I helped in the nursery at church, I wasn't prepared for the roomful of boundless energy. As soon as I set one child down from a table top, another one climbed into its place. No sooner had I stacked up the big blocks than a toddler delighted in scattering them about. The children were a picture of perpetual motion, exploring every nook and cranny.

But even with seemingly unlimited energy, their little bodies do run down. Despite their resistance, heavy eyelids droop, harder to open again after each blink, until finally they surrender to needed rest.

Can you imagine never getting tired? Never running out of strength? That's impossible, because a tired body stems from human weakness. Only God does not grow tired or weary.

Even growing toddlers become tired! But God alone is everlasting.

God renews our strength when we place our hope and faith in him. Instead of growing tired himself, God refreshes young and old alike.

When we depend daily on God and not on our own strength, he sustains us. Only God lasts through all time.

Yet you are enthroned as the Holy One; you are the praise of Israel. (Psalm 22:3)

Hold Me

Cast your cares on the LORD and he will sustain you; he will never let the righteous fall. (Psalm 55:22)

When my twin grandchildren, Alan and Mallory, began to string words into sentences, they sometimes twisted their intended messages. This resulted in scrambled meanings between what they thought and what they actually said.

The most captivating of their confused statements came when one or the other was in need of comfort or simply wanted companionship. They would entreat me with outstretched arms and pleading eyes, saying, "I need to hold you."

I needed no coaxing. I welcomed this opportunity to draw them close, to kiss scraped knees and elbows, and to give words of encouragement and love to scare away "monsters."

My grandchildren meant something other than what they actually said. But they had learned that when they voiced the words, "I need to hold you," someone would hold them. That was their goal. What they really thought, but could not verbalize, was, "Hold me, please. I need for you to make it better."

I recognize myself in their behavior. Just like Alan and Mallory, I need to share my hurts with someone who will give me unconditional love. My grandchildren trusted that I would help erase their troubles; likewise, I know that none of my problems are too great for God to handle.

I can take my burdens to God and tell him, "I need to hold you." Then, in the same way that I gather Alan and Mallory into my arms, God sustains me, giving hope and consolation. He opens his loving arms to me, and I move toward him, feeling the balm of his perfect love cover me.

Depend on God to kiss your hurts and scare away your monsters, whatever they may be. Place your trust in God's promises of comfort and care. Let him hold you.

Praise the LORD. Praise the LORD, O my soul. (Psalm 146:1)

Tracking Investments

"For where your treasure is, there your heart will be also."
(Matthew 6:21)

Have you checked on your investments lately? People check interest rates daily, watching the gains and losses.

This economical concern reminds me of a high school student whose dad gave her one hundred dollars. He instructed his daughter to buy stock in three companies of her choosing, which she did.

After that, early each morning, before going to her locker, she'd stop first in the school library. She'd take the *Wall Street Journal* from the newspaper rack, spread it on a table, and check out her stocks.

She kept track of her investments. She learned about her dividends, gaining proper direction for her future activity in the stock market.

God does pretty much the same as that student's dad. He gives us talents which we need to use wisely, in ways that please him. We can consult God's Wall Street Journal—the Holy Bible—for instructions on how to do this.

From the Ten Commandments (Exod. 20:1–17), to the Sermon on the Mount (Matt. 5–7), through the book of Revelation, God offers guidance and wisdom. We can be assured that his strength will sustain us whether our life's stock market moves up or down (Ps. 29:11; 46:1).

Just as that student did, we can establish our daily routine as the stock market players do. We can commune with God through praying, reading the Bible, and associating with other believers (Col. 4:2; Rom. 15:4; Heb. 10:25). The dividends will be worth our time!

Praise the LORD, O my soul, and forget not all his benefits. (Psalm 103:2)

Not Guilty!

"Abraham believed God, and it was credited to him as right-eousness." (Romans 4:3)

H ave you ever rushed to work, still half asleep, to push your time card into the clock or scoot behind your desk? You're out of breath but relieved you made it on time. You'll get your hours in today and receive full pay for the shift.

It's reassuring to know you'll collect wages for the number of hours worked. But how much more pleasing is the bonus check that comes not as something earned by hours of work but as a gift from an appreciative employer! And isn't it amazing how that bonus pay acts to motivate you to try to do a little better job for the boss?

That's the way it is with righteousness from God through Jesus Christ. Unlike a paycheck, righteousness cannot be earned. Instead, it's more like that bonus pay—God's gift.

Just as the bonus check results in added performance on the job, God's gift of righteousness results in our good works for him the same as it did for Abraham (James 2:14–26).

Because of our faith, God declares us righteous, free from sin. This "not guilty" verdict is for all who have faith in God through Christ.

I will give thanks to the LORD because of his righteous-ness and will sing praise to the name of the LORD Most High. (Psalm 7:17)

Reservations Confirmed

*"In my Father's house are many rooms; if it were not so,
I would have told you. I am going there to prepare a place for
you." (John 14:2)*

S tay at our house. . . . Your bedroom is ready!"
We planned to get a motel room while attending the family reunion. But now we were being urged to stay with relatives.

"But we don't want to crowd you," we protested.

"You won't crowd us. We have plenty of room."

This was a welcome invitation, for actually we hadn't looked forward to spending time in the motel room, separated from those we traveled to see. We all had a great weekend together.

God has made provision for an eternal reunion of his children. Jesus tells us about this heavenly get-together where God has prepared a place for all believers.

But if we want to share in that glorious reunion day, we need to prepare ourselves as worthy to meet in God's holy presence. This is possible through Jesus. He is our only way to experience God's forever family reunion.

*Through Jesus, therefore, let us continually offer to God
a sacrifice of praise. (Hebrews 13:15)*

5
WITNESS

Witness

Opportunities of Ministry for God

You completed the information on the entry form with casual interest. You dropped the slip of paper into the slot on top of the square box. Having forgotten all about entering the contest, you are surprised when the telephone call comes. You've won the grand prize—the trip of your dreams!

If this happened to you, what would you do even before you started packing your luggage? You probably wouldn't waste any time in telling someone about your good fortune. We usually want to share our pleasure. Good news begs to be told.

When we accept God's invitation to salvation through his Son, Jesus Christ, and when we learn to expect and receive God's providential care, then we have good news that we want to share. We want to introduce our new Shepherd to our family and friends. We want even strangers to know who Jesus is and what he is able to bring into a life.

Opportunities to share the Good News of Jesus will come our way daily. Some of these chances will be obvious; however, there will be other opportunities which we may never recognize. Times when we will influence people by what we say or do. In business or social contacts we may attract the attention of those whom God wants to hear his message.

When you read the following selections, I hope you will gain an understanding that we are God's witnesses every day. I pray you will be a genuine witness for God through your lifestyle.

Night-Light Security

"Let your light shine before men, that they may see your good deeds and praise your Father in heaven." (Matthew 5:16)

As a youngster, I needed a light left on at night. Its small beam relieved my fears of the dark and helped me to sleep in peace.

I now depend on the comforting glow of God's protection whenever I'm in the dark. And in turn I can reflect his brilliance to those around me. If I maintain my prayer life and study of his Word, others can see Jesus through me. I can be God's guide for those searching for truth. My light can be as piercing as the lighthouse beacon slicing through the black of a night's storm. I don't want temptations or evil habits to spoil my witness for God. I want my light to point a path to God so that he will be praised (Matt. 5:16).

I cherish the memory of that childhood night-light's security. It encourages me to leave a spiritual light on for others. A light to brighten their way to God while they struggle through Satan's concealing darkness.

For God is the King of all the earth; sing to him a psalm of praise. (Psalm 47:7)

OBEYING THE COACH

Do nothing out of selfish ambition. (Philippians 2:3)

When he was twelve years old, my son, Brian, stood at second base when a teammate came to bat with two outs. At the crack of the bat, Brian sprang from second base, his one goal to reach third. Halfway there he saw his coach waving him on, yelling, "Don't stop, go for home." I don't know which moved faster, the windmill motion of the coach's arm or my son's legs as he rounded third base.

His speed forced Brian into a wide turn, but finally my son straightened his path, arms and legs pumping and head bobbing. He made it home, but not before the ball.

Before the dust around home plate had settled, the coach was at Brian's side, draped his big arm around the boy's slumped shoulders and praised his effort. You see, my son would rather have stopped in safety at third base. But he put aside his selfish goal of staying on third and instead obeyed his coach. The coach called him "coachable," valuable for future games.

Often God urges us to follow him in ways we'd rather not go. We really don't relish going out on visitation night for our church to speak to strangers. Sometimes it's not a pleasure going to see those sick in the hospital, or taking food by their home. We'd rather stay in the comfort of third base.

At times I'd rather hold on to my own goals instead of yielding to God's will. But to be a valuable player in God's game of life requires that I obey him. Those who watch me will know when I follow his direction and guidance.

I will be glad and rejoice in you; I will sing praise to your name, O Most High. (Psalm 9:2)

Faith Testimony

"I have found you righteous in this generation." (Genesis 7:1)

Hurricane Andrew stormed across southern Florida in 1992, leaving thousands homeless. TV newscasts showed street after street of flattened houses. A few withstood the strong winds because their construction met required building codes. Spared, these houses were testimonies to their builders' integrity.

In Noah's day, sin's corruption and violence swept through the earth. But even as God prepared to destroy the evil, God chose to spare Noah. God considered Noah righteous, rewarding him with the promised covenant.

Much like those well-built houses in Hurricane Andrew's path, Noah's faith didn't falter. He did exactly as God told him. Building the ark served as Noah's testimony of his faith and obedience to God. The results reinforced his faith.

Tolerance is coming to mean not only acceptance of all people but also of their differing beliefs as correct. Jesus loved sinners but was not tolerant of their behavior.

When we're expected to embrace that which is contrary to God's laws, we face a true test of our faith. Will we protest when our co-workers encourage someone to have an abortion? Will we stop the spread of untrue gossip (is there any other kind)? When drugs are passed around our social gathering, will we timidly stand up for our principles?

Will we speak out in agreement with the Scriptures?

What would Jesus do?

If we take an unfaltering stand for God and his purpose, as Noah did, God will reward our faithful witness to him.

You who fear the Lord, praise him! (Psalm 22:23)

Correct Name Tags

How great is the love the Father has lavished on us, that we should be called children of God! (1 John 3:1)

Nursery workers at my church write each baby's name on masking tape and stick it to the back of the baby's clothes.

When we become Christians, we take the name of Christ as spiritual identification. Even though Christ doesn't slap a wide strip of masking tape across our backs labeling us as his, our community and the world will recognize us for whose we are.

People can see that we are different when we refuse to become a party to frivolous worldly pleasures that break God's laws. When we don't choose fleeting delights as our foundations for living, the world knows we place our dependence on the solid rock of Jesus.

We have joy in being aligned with God. When the world around us seems to lose its godly values and forsake proven virtues, we are grounded in God. His promises are everlasting.

Jesus teaches that a tree can be identified by its fruit (Matt. 7:20). In the same manner, the fruits of the Holy Spirit are colorful Christian name tags (Gal. 5:22–23).

We choose to put on God's label. May we live up to the expectations of those wearing the Christian name tag.

Let them praise your great and awesome name. (Psalm 99:3)

Proper Places

"Seek first his kingdom." (Matthew 6:33)

Do you remember playing Chinese checkers? Sometimes you'd have almost all your marbles to the other side when someone would bump the board. Marbles would roll every which way. The game couldn't continue until each marble was again in its proper place.

Isn't that like what happens now and then in the Christian life? When we cheat a little on our giving to God, holding back some for ourselves, what sometimes happens? That little extra we thought we'd have goes for some unexpected thing like unplugging the drain or replacing the broken window. When we abandon God's priorities, everything gets all mixed up like those rolling marbles.

When we give God his proper place in our life, he puts everything back in order. Then our days will be ready to be lived as God planned, bathed with his joy, peace, and love.

I will exalt you, my God the King; I will praise your name for ever and ever. (Psalm 145:1)

Back in Business

And God is able to make all grace abound to you, so that in
all things . . . you will abound in every good work.
(2 Corinthians 9:8)

Relaxing in my den one July afternoon, I glanced out the window to discover my colorful impatiens weeping for attention. The scorching heat had drained the tiny flowers and leaves into withering ugliness. Choking in the high humidity, the flowers begged for their daily watering I'd missed yesterday and today.

Pushing fatigue aside, I rushed outside to their rescue. I let the garden hose's thin spray gently cool the plant, drench its soil and soak deep around it roots. I continued until the hanging basket overflowed, water splattering onto the parched ground below.

After supper I checked on them. To my delight, the flowers which had drooped their heads near death a few hours earlier, had perked up like it was the cool of an early spring morning. They'd become their old selves, displaying vivid pinks, reds, and lavenders as proudly as ever before. They were back in their business of adding beauty to their surroundings.

I was reminded how the same thing can bring us down in our Christian living. If we neglect our commitment to God, even for a day or two, we give Satan the opportunity he's waiting for to destroy us (1 Pet. 5:8). When we don't do daily Bible study, meditate with God, and spend time in prayer with him, we're neglecting necessary maintenance of a Spirit-filled life.

Just as I didn't care properly for my impatiens, if we don't tend our relationship with God on a regular basis, we'll have to start a rescue procedure. We'll have to renew our efforts, get back in a balanced lifestyle with Christ.

But it can be done. My wilting impatiens revived when they received what they needed. They again burst forth, fulfilling their purpose of creation.

Without God's daily sustaining power, we will fall short of God's purpose for us. We will wilt when facing temptations and disappointments. However, we can actively pursue his direction by listening to his voice through the Bible (Col. 3:16), through prayer (Rom. 12:12), through fellowship with other believers (Heb. 10:25), and through praise music (Eph. 5: 19–20).

We don't have to spend our days in wilting uselessness for God. God can refresh us like he did the woman at the well (John 4:13–14). His grace is sufficient for us (2 Cor. 9:8), but we must seek that grace (Heb. 4:16). Then, like my flowers, we can be back in business with God, living as he intended. We can again be God's effective witness, adding the beauty of his message to our surroundings.

My tongue will speak of your righteousness and of your praises all day long. (Psalm 35:28)

Altered Images

We are therefore Christ's ambassadors, as though God were making his appeal through us. (2 Corinthians 5:20)

Did you ever go through a "fun house" at the fair? Those places certainly gave reason for a lot of laughs. Especially the strange mirrors.

Standing before them, people appeared taller, wider, shorter, or skinnier than in reality. The mirrors were not trustworthy; therefore the images they produced were inaccurate. Sometimes a person was difficult to recognize from their reflection.

Do our lives mirror to the world an accurate likeness of God? Or are we a pillar of the community in our church pew on Sunday, but give our other six days to Satan? Do we behave as a model parent at PTA meetings and then sprout horns in the bleachers, screaming abuse at the Little League umpire?

Do we project a faithful representation of Jesus Christ or an altered image?

I will praise you, O Lord my God, with all my heart; I will glorify your name forever. (Psalm 86:12)

Camera Ready

Create in me a pure heart, O God, and renew a steadfast spirit within me. (Psalm 51:10)

My eyes serve me like a camera, clicking away on an endless roll of film. Each evening my mind develops the snapshots, and I discover my day's mood stamped across them.

On stressful days, it's obvious my impatience has spread intimidation across my sweet child's face. Pictures taken on difficult days reveal a loving husband, now reserved, letting me pour out my frustrations on him simply because he's there.

Images from these warped days unveil store clerks, bag boys, and even neighbors, perplexed at how to handle me. They withdraw from my nearness, their faces lined with uneasiness.

Confronted by my camera's disclosures, I declare my shame before God. Sleep overtakes me as I seek God's forgiveness for not being his approved witness today.

After such an imperfect day, I awake the next morning asking God to cleanse my heart, knowing it's the wellspring of life.

Maybe today I'll see my child's bright eyes that, yesterday, clouds of my impatience darkened. Today I'll speak more kindly to my husband and see his relief as I hold my tongue. Perhaps my smile today will signal store clerks, bag boys, and neighbors they don't have to cross to the other side of the street when they see me coming.

Tonight, before I surrender to sleep, I'll thank God for loving me no matter what my mood. God knows and tests my heart. His unconditional love can equip me to meet every day. God's joy can make me camera-ready so that my daily pictures will please him.

Praise the LORD. How good it is to sing praises to our God, how pleasant and fitting to praise him! (Psalm 147:1)

Winds of Doubt

He who doubts is like a wave of the sea, blown and tossed by the wind. (James 1:6)

At the seashore, I'm content watching waves tumble toward the beach, pushing their foamy trails across the sand. Occasionally I track a particular wave's difficult journey inland as the wind alters its course. The wave changes directions until bigger waves finally swallow it completely.

God warns that doubt will have similar consequences in our spiritual lives. Have you been a Christian so long that you've lost the zing in your relationship with God? Or are you a new Christian and already you wonder what you were thinking about when you walked that aisle and gave your heart to Jesus? Don't get trapped on doubt's one way street. Recall the commitment you made to God. Read again those Scriptures that brought you to God's saving grace and let them strengthen anew your spiritual resolve (Rom. 3:23; 5:8; 6:23; 10:9,13). Don't leave room in your heart for doubt.

The Bible labels people "double-minded" when doubt holds a stronger foothold than faith in their lives. The Bible also compares a doubter with a wind-tossed wave at the seashore. James calls this person "unstable in all he does" (James 1:8). Spiritual doubt reaps compromise and defeat.

Like big waves gobble up smaller ones, Satan plants his seeds of doubt, trying to replace God in our lives. We can safeguard our commitment to God by strapping on his full armor. Equipped for battle, we can then fight the elements of doubt Satan blows our way (Eph. 6:11–17).

Praise be to the Lord, the God of Israel, from everlasting to everlasting. (Psalm 106:48)

BEARING HIS IMPRINT

"I have engraved you on the palms of my hands." (Isaiah 49:16)

"Out of sight, out of mind," sometimes proves prophetic when great distances separate acquaintances. Promises to keep in touch dim with time.

Not so with God.

God promises not to forget Israel. What a great statement of comfort from God!

The promise of remembrance from the Old Testament extends to us. From the engravings of the Israelites on God's palms to the nails thrust into the palms of Jesus' hands, God's love for us remains ever-evident.

What about our love for him? Is it just as obvious? Do we have God engraved on us? Do we extend love without partiality as Jesus did to both Jew and Gentile? Do we forgive those who wrong us as Jesus did on the cross? Do we accept our rebellious children as Jesus taught in the parable of the prodigal son?

May we strive to live Christlike lives, bearing his imprint as a witness to God's promised love and salvation.

I will bow down toward your holy temple and will praise your name for your love and your faithfulness. (Psalm 138:2)

6

RELATIONSHIPS

Relationships

INFLUENCE OF GOD'S UNCONDITIONAL LOVE

A ssault against the family to undermine its peace and tranquility is not unique to modern day living. Generation gaps and rebellious children are nothing new.

The Bible's first family was mightily assailed, and staggered under the blows of Satan. When Adam and Eve yielded to Satan's temptation in the Garden of Eden, the first incident of marital discord appeared: they couldn't agree on whose fault it was that they had eaten of the forbidden fruit (Gen. 3:11–13).

From its beginning, Adam and Eve's family struggled with ample troubles. The first crime statistic occurred when one of their boys murdered the other (Gen. 4:8).

Prostitution, adultery, slander, hatred, jealousy—we could go on and on. These perplexing complications in life did not start with our generation. The Bible records time after time when bonds between people were marred by these and other problems. Problems that continue to rip open the seams of relationships.

Do you value companionships? What measures would you go to in order to preserve a friendship? Do you take quick steps to mend shaky alliances?

Remember all the loving associations Jesus formed? Lazarus, Mary, and Martha; his twelve closest companions, the disciples; the leper; the blind; the demon-possessed; the sinner; even Judas Iscariot, his betrayer. Jesus loved each of them with the boundless love of his Father.

God's love overlooks every outward blemish or fault. It doesn't matter to God what we have done, whether we're good looking or have a perfect figure. God projects his love beyond all the imperfections and into an individual's heart.

Talking about God without mentioning his love is like trusting a two-legged chair to support you. In both cases something is missing. God is love (1 John 4:16). Without God there is no healing or forgiveness to salve the open wounds in severed relationships. Without his love, people can't get past the outward appearances of others.

But with God's love, we can love even persons we dislike. Recognizing that God loves us, we can reflect it to those around us; to family, friends, and acquaintances. We can allow the influence of God's unconditional love to flow through us and into every relationship we have.

I pray the following selections convince you that having God's love in your heart can inspire your every association. His constant love and acceptance can bathe all your relationships with God's precious peace.

It's Not a Choice

"This is my command: Love each other." (John 15:17)

God's Word commands us to love (John 15:12). If we are obedient, to love is not a choice.

The educated men of Jesus' day sought to confuse him with their questions (Matt. 22:34–40; Mark 12:28–31). An expert in the law asked Jesus which was the most important of all the commandments.

His answer left no doubt: The greatest commandment is to love God and the second greatest is to love your neighbor. Loving God first and others second puts the right order of importance in our lives. All other concerns rest on this priority of our love.

These two commandments direct us to love God with all our heart, soul, mind, and strength and then to love our neighbor as ourself. Jesus' sacrificial life reveals the perfect example of this powerful love. He walked in love and gave his life for us (Eph. 5:2).

Just what is this love that springs so easily from the hearts of God the Father and Jesus the Son? How can we possibly meet the demands to produce such a love for God and especially for others? Where do we start? Where is the source of such emotion?

God wrapped his greatest gift to the world in this unconditional love. Jesus presented himself through life and death as his Father's love offering. God is the source of love.

Scripture supplies instruction about what love is in 1 Corinthians 13. There, in simple, certain terms is the recipe for Christian love for one another.

God says love does not envy, does not boast, is not proud. It is not rude or self-seeking, or easily angered, and doesn't remember wrongs done to it. Love finds no delight in evil, but favors truth instead. God describes love as patient and kind. It always protects and always trusts its object of affection. Love always hopes; it always endures. Love never fails.

Always. Never. God uses these two words that imply permanence when describing his greatest gift—love. He's able to give us this kind of wonderful love and, in turn, enable us to give each other the same kind of love.

A friend's new mother-in-law wasn't at all happy with her son's choice for a wife. The older woman made no secret of her feelings, which became an unkind barrier to every courteous gesture from my friend.

Finally, my friend's approach to her disapproving mother-in-law was, "I'll just love her with God's love." She repaid the woman's harsh criticisms with kindness; she held her anger when provoked; she didn't keep track of how many times her mother-in-law put her down but instead always remained patient. That unconditional, Christian love described in 1 Corinthians 13 broke through the wall and paved a path toward a lasting relationship between the two women.

Have life's assaults slapped you around until you feel unloved and incapable of loving? Do you think your life is broken beyond repair? Let God apply the strong glue of his love to every piece of it. When you surrender your brokenness to him, he picks you up and makes you a beautiful vessel as the potter molds a perfect bowl from a clump of clay. Let his love saturate your every thought, word, and deed. Then, with your life held together by God's unconditional love, you can first love him and then love others.

"I thank you and praise you, O God of my fathers."
(Daniel 2:23)

Quick to Ask, Slow to Give?

Pray . . . on all occasions with all kinds of prayers and requests. (Ephesians 6:18)

Our prayers tend to be more intense when we find ourselves in troublesome situations. We want to eliminate what distresses us, especially if it affects us personally.

The child doesn't receive an invitation to the party and his mother quickly asks God to soothe the child's pain. The teenager doesn't make the cheerleading squad or the basketball team and her parents pray to God for help to bolster self-esteem and patience. And, of course, in times of sickness or death of a dear friend or family member, we draw closer to God in search of comfort.

When facing difficulties, we sometimes are quicker to ask of God than we are to give to God our praise, thanks, honor, and adoration.

Even Jesus, who never neglected communion with his Father, fervently prayed in Gethsemane, "take this cup from me" (Luke 22:42). Yes, even Jesus, at that dark hour on the Mount of Olives, asked God for relief.

Jesus conversed with his Father that day: "Father, if you are willing, take this cup from me; yet not my will, but yours be done" (Luke 22:42). Jesus further submits to his Father while praying a second and third time the same day: "My Father, if it is not possible for this cup to be taken away unless I drink it, may your will be done" (Matt. 26:42–43).

In our efforts to be more Christlike in our praying, may we sincerely pray the words of Jesus, "I do not seek my own will but the will of the Father" (John 5:30 NKJV).

God encourages us to petition him at any time with our needs and desires. The inspired word from God through Paul in Ephesians 6:18 instructs us about our praying: "Pray in the Spirit on all occasions with all kinds of prayers and requests." And in Philippians 4:6, Paul tells us, "present your requests to God." So, God's Word teaches us we may pray to our Heavenly Father on any occasion, presenting him with whatever request we choose.

Before we consider prayer as anything less than precious communication with God, let's remember John's words—"This is the confidence we have in approaching God: that if we ask anything according to his will, he hears us" (1 John 5:14). That's how his Son prayed from Gethsemane, according to his will. What a wondrous model for our prayers!

We are not only taught to pray according to his will. God's Word also instructs us to approach him prayerfully on more than an as-needed basis: "Devote yourselves to prayer, being watchful and thankful" (Col. 4:2). "Pray continually" (1 Thess. 5:17). God desires our communication with him. He created us for himself (Col. 1:16). He teaches persistent petitions and praise, day and night (Luke 18:1–8).

If we maintain this regular, sincere prayer position with God, we will be comfortable going to him any time, especially when troubled.

I urged my children from a very early age to make time each day for talking with God in prayer. How sad I would be, I told them, if they didn't talk to me all day, maybe for several days, just to share with me their good feelings as well as their problems. Then I told them God would also be saddened when one of his children did not share their life with him by talking to him every day.

In God we make our boast all day long, and we will praise your name forever. (Psalm 44:8)

Able to Share

For this reason I kneel before the Father, from whom his whole family in heaven and on earth derives its name. (Ephesians 3:14–15)

O ther kids seemed to envy my not having to share my toys with brothers and sisters. My teenage peers thought it neat that I didn't have to share my bed and bath. And I suppose some adults think I'm lucky not having to share whatever wealth my parents may leave.

Not experiencing sibling rivalry, I suppose I took for granted having showers of love from two parents at all times.

Recently while expressing thanksgiving to God for his peace in my life, I was suddenly aware that he treats me special, as if I'm his only child. God downplays the fact that he has thousands of children. And he never compares me with any of them. He always gives me his undivided attention.

I feel special being treated like an only child by my Heavenly Father. And I don't need earthly siblings to be able to share this feeling!

Let everything that has breath praise the LORD. Praise the LORD. (Psalm 150:6)

You Can't Turn Back

"Let the little children come to me, and do not hinder them."
(Matthew 19:14)

A newspaper clipping, now yellowed with age, expresses a universal feeling shared by parents everywhere.

It's an *Arlo and Janis* cartoon strip. After sending his grumbling young son from the room, Arlo, the father, stands alone, deep in bewildered thought. In the last two frames of the cartoon Arlo explains his feelings to his wife: "Having kids is like jumping from an airplane. You don't know exactly where you're heading but you can't turn back!"

This echoes the opinion that being a parent is the most difficult job in the world. People doing the least difficult tasks in our society must submit to a few hours of job training; yet, the enormous occupation of parenting requires none.

When it comes to raising precious children, many parents walk a daily tightrope. New parents listen to ready advice from anyone, only to discover what worked with one baby won't work for theirs. Later, they learn that successful discipline for one family makes no difference in the behavior of their child.

Distressed parents buy this book and that book, searching for solutions to fit their problems. Parenting books overflow their bookshelves. I wonder whether these frustrated and sometimes scared parents have read the bestseller of them all. From reading the Bible, parents can glean God's wisdom for their parenting tasks.

Proverbs 22:6 urges parents to "train a child in the way he should go, and when he is old he will not turn from it." How can we accomplish this? The Bible encourages us to begin by example, with love and tenderness: "Do not exasperate your children; instead, bring them up in the training and instruction of the Lord" (Eph. 6:4).

This training and instruction of the Lord involves spiritual teaching. When Moses reveals the Ten Commandments to the people of Israel, he says: "These commandments that I give you today are to be upon your hearts. Impress them on your children. Talk about them when you sit at home and when you walk along the road, when you lie down and when you get up" (Deut. 6:6–7). So, we're to bring up our children with daily mention of the words of God, his commandments, his love.

Many, many times Scripture teaches intercessory prayer (e.g., Eph. 6:18; James 5:16); in fact, Jesus prayed for his disciples and for all believers (John 17). Therefore, we're to pray for our children. Paul prays for the Christians at Colosse with a prayer I've prayed often for my children (Col. 1:9–12). It is an appropriate prayer to offer for anyone, even for ourselves.

Following Paul's prayer as a guide, I don't stop praying for my children: I ask God to give them spiritual wisdom and understanding of his will for their lives. I pray my children may live worthy of God and please him in every way, being fruitful in good works, and growing in their knowledge of God. My prayer is that God will strengthen them with his might and glorious power. I pray they may have patience and endurance coupled with joyful thanks to God for their inheritance into his kingdom.

In spite of all our best efforts, we won't be perfect parents. Nor will we have perfect children. As long as we're exposed to Satan's temptations in the world around us, both we and our children will sometimes fall short of our goals. All the more reason our prayers should never cease! For our children and for ourselves.

All children are different by nature. Remember Isaac's twin sons: "The boys grew up, and Esau became a skillful hunter, a man of the open country, while Jacob was a quiet man, staying among the tents" (Gen. 25:27).

Keeping this in mind, we know our methods of nurture and association with each child will necessarily differ. But we continue to teach them the ways of God, and we don't stop praying for each of them.

Once a parent, we're always a parent. As children move through stages and ages, parenting takes on different assignments. Whether a new parent or one whose nest is empty, we can continue to apply the same biblical instructions throughout our children's lives.

"Yours, O LORD, is the greatness and the power and the glory and the majesty and the splendor, for everything in heaven and earth is yours." (1 Chronicles 29:11)

Gold Mining

Humble yourselves before the Lord, and he will lift you up.
(James 4:10)

I've accepted the fact that Ed McMahon won't ever phone me and I don't have a rich uncle. But, I have children—the gold mines God put in my life. Although our two children grew up in the same family, they're as different as baked potatoes and French fries.

My older child blossomed from puberty into adolescence and teenage years in the seventies. She was as open as the books I read to her, sharing her hopes, dreams, tears, and fears. Our talks were more her talking and me listening, giving her a sounding board for her frustrations and problems. We didn't always find solutions, but the time spent together searching for them served its good purpose for each of us.

On the other hand, my second child took his first steps pulling against the helping hand I offered. As he burst into his teenage years in the eighties, family traditions paled in the glow of the independence his driver's license afforded him. I watched him rush to become a free spirit, straining at every restriction.

I thank God daily for giving me children, however different they are, and for enough love and patience to have cared for them. And aren't the circumstances similar concerning God and his children? We're all different, yet God recognizes and deals with those differences one individual at a time.

When we hurt too much to share, God waits patiently until we approach him with our burden. When our frustrations mount, God knows our thoughts and longs for us to spend time with him, looking at the solutions he offers.

All you have made will praise you, O Lord. (Psalm 145:10)

THE YO-YO SYNDROME

His love endures forever. (Psalm 136:1)

Have you ever cut a yo-yo string? You know the one. Its strength sometimes rivals that of the apron strings.

The almost-grown, dependent teenager uses the yo-yo string quite effectively. Just a slight pull brings the willing parent closer into the teenager's life when there's a need the parent can supply.

But when no further immediate need exists, the child pushes the perplexed parent away. The parent then walks around as if on eggshells, not wanting to irritate the teenager. Let a sleeping dog lie, you know.

It's lonesome out there at the end of the yo-yo string. Parents long to fellowship with their child, but the "no vacancy" sign shines brightly. So parents pass on by, happy to receive their teen's occasional nod.

This pull-in, push-away procedure repeats itself as needs arise or attitudes sour. The child plays the parent like a yo-yo.

But at the far end of the string, a parent wonders, *Who's in charge here? I'm the parent. I should be in charge, shouldn't I?* Parents are tempted to throw back their shoulders and walk around the house like it was theirs.

Tired of being used, parents promise themselves, *That's the last time that child will yank me around.* They decide to return like attitude, ignoring their teenager.

But usually that plan doesn't work. Parents end up feeling as if they owe an apology for giving the child the silent treatment.

"M-o-m-m-m-m-m-m-m," the wailing voice pierces the air, luring the parent to the bedroom door.

"Mom, I'm missing a button on my shirt, and I've got to wear it tonight. They're picking me up in ten minutes. You've got to fix it!"

No other shirt will do, of course. Moms don't even ask.

"Sure, which button's missing, honey?"

The tug of the taut yo-yo string pulls Mom into the room. As she reaches for the shirt, she drapes her loving apron strings around the teenager.

I wonder if that child's behavior reflects my own relationship with God. Do I keep God at the end of a yo-yo string so I can reel him near whenever I need him?

Talking with God sometimes loses its importance when our lives flow smoothly. But at first storm warnings, we cry out, "Father!" We need only call once. He's waiting to be a part of our daily lives.

God has apron strings, too. When we become his children, he lovingly drapes those apron strings around us, binding us to him and his eternal care. We're the ones who untie God's apron strings. We're the ones who shed God's ways and wander away from him.

But, just like the parent of a sometimes ungrateful child, God waits for our return. He's at our heart's door, ready to retie the apron strings.

Therefore I will praise you among the nations, O LORD;
I will sing praises to your name. (Psalm 18:49)

Sticks and Stones

Set a guard over my mouth, O Lord; keep watch over the door of my lips. (Psalm 141:3)

During his earthly ministry, Jesus was in the business of forgiveness through repentance: "I have not come to call the righteous, but sinners" (Matt. 9:13). He continues that same forgiving ministry today.

When the scribes and Pharisees brought before Jesus a woman caught in adultery, they wanted him to condemn her to death by stoning. Jesus reverses the situation on them by replying, "If any one of you is without sin, let him be the first to throw a stone at her" (John 8:7). After the crowd leaves without throwing one stone, Jesus asks the woman, "Has no one condemned you?" (John 8:10). To her reply of "No one, sir," Jesus responds, "Neither do I condemn you" (John 8:11).

That group of scribes and Pharisees realized they were not sinless and therefore unqualified to assign guilt to anyone else.

Today, humankind still falls short of perfection, not at all qualified to dispense condemning criticism of another. Even being perfect, Jesus gave mercy, not criticism, to the adulterous woman.

Jesus admonishes, "Do to others as you would have them do to you" (Luke 6:31). Where else could this Golden Rule apply as appropriately than the area of criticism?

Do we enjoy hearing criticism aimed at us? How do we feel when someone heaps blame on us? Wouldn't we rather they upheld us instead? From childhood through old age, people bloom more favorably in the complimentary shower of praise than in the drought of constant criticism.

If we tend to take a too-critical approach to others, we can remember the Golden Rule. Doing so will encourage us to think about how our own words would sound if directed to ourselves.

Perfection lies beyond anyone's grasp. What good purpose exists to being critical of another's imperfection? A better approach in any relationship would be to "encourage one another and build each other up" (1 Thess. 5:11).

Children chant the familiar rhyme, "Sticks and stones may break my bones, but words will never hurt me." What a mistaken notion! We need to weigh every critical thought lest the resulting words cause hurt.

Following his teaching of the Beatitudes, Jesus advises, "Be merciful, just as your Father is merciful. Do not judge. . . . Do not condemn" (Luke 6:36–37).

Praise the LORD, O my soul; all my inmost being, praise his holy name. (Psalm 103:1)

ENOUGH LOVE

The grace of our Lord was poured out on me abundantly,
along with the faith and love that are in Christ Jesus.
(1 Timothy 1:14)

People buzzed about their grandchildren; I couldn't understand their enthusiasm. I wondered what could demand that much interest. I watched them surrender to silliness. I listened as grownups regressed into an infantile state.

"Never," I declared, "will I become that immature. I'll never utter senseless baby talk to something so tiny and underdeveloped. It's not even aware of my existence!"

These words came from me, who in recent years chose tables in restaurants a good distance from small children.

But I made all those protests before the appearance of my first grandchildren. Yes, grand*children*, because God blessed me with two on the same date: twins—a boy and a girl.

My first glimpse of them came when they were en route from the delivery room to their accommodations in the hospital nursery. Two tiny wrinkled bundles of miracle. And, oh, what a tug at my heart! Unfamiliar emotions surfaced at that predawn hour, and a space in my heart I didn't know was empty filled with a delightful warmth.

With each passing month of their young lives, they both became mobile, were intelligent (of course), and didn't miss much of what went on around them.

When I visited their home, I'd go inside to discover them still as mice, their activity stopped in midair, both looking expectantly toward the door to see who had knocked. Two steps inside, I'd usually set my bundles down and drop to my knees.

I was rewarded with two big smiles as they started toward me and walked into my open, outstretched arms.

I hugged them, wondering whether I'd have enough love for both at the same time; I've realized I do.

I wanted to cling to them as long as possible. But a few seconds and they squirmed to be released. I reluctantly let the toddlers move away, hoping they would share more of themselves during my visit.

This little greeting custom my grandchildren and I established reminds me of how we can move into the calm of God's loving arms. He's always ready to be our Friend (Rev. 3:20). Then, like I do with my twin grandchildren, God gives us our coveted freedom and patiently waits for our return to a closeness with him. He has enough love for all of us.

Sing praises to God, sing praises; sing praises to our King, sing praises. (Psalm 47:6)

SOMETHING LIKE GARDENING

Let us not become weary in doing good, for at the proper time
we will reap a harvest if we do not give up. (Galatians 6:9)

My gardening talents are limited to growing weeds in the springtime. One fall, longing for some color in my yard to brighten winter days ahead, I bought a flat of pansies. A plastic tag stuck into their dirt promised red blooms from every little sprout.

With the excitement of a first-time gardener, I carefully moved the tiny plants to prominent places around my home. Some went into flower pots adorning the deck, some occupied a large planter on the front porch, and a few came to rest in the ground as a border near my back door.

The same sun shone on them all; rain that fell in the front yard also watered the backyard. Not one plant died! But while some pansies bloomed a deep, velvety red, others didn't produce even a hint of color.

I wondered what I'd done wrong. Even though I'd given the same kind and amount of care to each one, some fulfilled my expectations and others did not.

As I reflect on my half-successful flower gardening, I'm reminded that life is sometimes the same: some people will meet our expectations and some will not.

I have an acquaintance whose mood never quite catches up with the stream of our conversations. She seems content for our children to play together, but lacks enthusiasm for what's going on around her. Regardless of my efforts to coax her into a friendship, she remains on the outside of our circle of friends, sharing only an occasional smile, but expresses no desire for real involvement.

My hopes that year for blooms in the border near my back door went unfulfilled. But I decided to try my luck with pansies again the next fall. We can continue to be Christlike and keep on trying in our relationships with people, too.

I will praise God's name in song and glorify him with thanksgiving. (Psalm 69:30)

Never Paid in Full

Love does no harm to its neighbor. Therefore love is the fulfillment of the law. (Romans 13:10)

We can't help smiling when we make our last car payment. Even churches sometimes commemorate the full payment of a building debt with a "burn the mortgage" celebration.

A Christian's debt of love can never be paid in full because it is a God-given continuing debt.

God instructs us to love our neighbor as fulfillment of his law. In the parable of the Good Samaritan (Luke 10:25–37), Jesus defined our neighbor as anyone in need.

Not only does this Golden Rule of love fulfill the law, it holds all else together. Love even underlies our obeying civil authorities and laws.

Love will not harm a neighbor. Instead, all of God's commandments are bound up in his instruction to love. Loving our neighbor as ourself is a necessary step toward abiding by God's laws governing Christian living.

I looked forward to a new neighbor moving onto our street. I had heard of their community involvement and had seen their pictures in the newspaper supporting worthy causes. I fully expected them to be receptive to me when I walked over to welcome them into our neighborhood. The reverse proved true as they gave me a cool nod, listened to me prattle on, and then bid me farewell with no hint of being glad I'd been there. As the months pass I wave to them when I drive by, and they only stare with little response.

But God's command to love my neighbor still stands. God's love can help me break through their reserve. God expects me to share his love with them and with his help for boldness, I will continue to show these folks neighborly love. That's a love debt I owe to God.

> *It is good to praise the* LORD *and make music to your name, O Most High, to proclaim your love in the morning, and your faithfulness at night. (Psalm 92:1)*

7
PRAISE

Praise

A Love Relationship With Jesus

In a love relationship, certain elements are necessary for that union to survive: A total commitment of loyalty; a desire to please another; happiness and contentment just to be in the presence of the one we love.

Reading through these pages, have you realized that God desires those same feelings from you when you cultivate a love relationship with him? I hope each group of meditations has helped you to progressively discover God's greatness.

Have you looked inward at the way you regard life? I hope you have confirmed that even in the worst of times, God can be found in the circumstances when you seek a proper perspective. Once you acknowledge God's presence, your commitment to him will call for your every effort to maintain a harmonious relationship with a holy God.

God gives abundant provision and security to those who love him and obey him. God expects us to tell others about him, making the most of our witness opportunities. All our relationships will thrive when watered by the pleasant warmth of his unconditional love.

The sum of these discoveries about God will flow naturally into this final section about giving praise and thanksgiving to him. Please don't settle for having a religion without a relationship with Jesus. You cannot inherit this relationship from your family or gain it through a church membership. It's a one-on-one, personal encounter with Jesus Christ.

No one can meet Jesus for you; he accepts no substitutes. It's up to you to call upon Jesus to be your Savior and your Lord (Rom. 9:9,13). Having done so, don't be ashamed to praise him for what he does in your life. When you acknowledge Jesus to others, he will also tell his Father about you (Matt. 10:32–33).

May you read the following pages with a heart full of praise for the awesome majesty of God.

Behold His Glory

The heavens declare the glory of God; the skies proclaim the work of his hands. (Psalm 19:1)

Fifteen and a brand new Christian, I'd never attended a sunrise church service. Indeed, I'd never even seen a sunrise. At a church retreat in the Great Smoky Mountains, I got my opportunity.

An hour before the sun rose our group of sleepy pilgrims met. In the predawn haze, I hiked a short distance down the road before crossing an open field. I left an irregular path of footprints on its dew-bathed grass. I followed the guide as the terrain steepened.

Making my way up the narrow trail, I reached a clearing on the hilltop. After a short devotional, I silently waited. I'd heard others praise this moment as a unique, transforming adventure.

God's paint brush moved with flawless perfection. He streaked the sky with startling pinks and flaming reds to announce the day's impending arrival. Yellows and oranges spilled from his palette and flooded the landscape. The regal fireball peeked above the distant mountain's outline.

Instantly my worldly concerns vanished, and I experienced genuine renewing of the mind. I keenly felt the Lord's presence and identified with John: "The Word became flesh and made his dwelling among us. We have seen his glory" (John 1:14).

I witnessed one of God's great and glorious miracles of renewal that early morning. Since then, I've been privileged to enjoy other sunrises from mountains and seashores. But if I'm never blessed with the sight of another one, I won't feel deprived. My memory of that one remains as detailed as if it happened this morning. Recalling it draws me closer to God and the knowledge of his omnipresence to sustain me.

Let heaven and earth praise him, the seas and all that move in them. (Psalm 69:34)

Like Elevator Music

"You will rejoice, and no one will take away your joy."
(John 16:22)

A re you a happy person?

"Of course I am," you might reply. Or perhaps you'd answer, "Most of the time." Then on second thought, "Well, sometimes." Further thought may reveal that your happy times don't last. They come and go.

Don't we all know people who appear happy no matter what their changing situations? No setback dampens their excitement. Their pleasure overflows. Events don't govern the degree of their happiness. What resource do these people draw from when times turn sour?

After listing how wrong things could go, Habakkuk says in his hymn of faith that despite the bad times, "yet I will rejoice in the LORD, I will joy in the God of my salvation" (Hab. 3:18 NKJV). David declares to God, "You will fill me with joy in your presence, with eternal pleasures at your right hand" (Ps. 16:11).

Eternal. God's gifts are not temporary, consumed today and gone forever. Whatever God offers—strength, peace, hope, love, encouragement, protection—is permanent and promised to those who believe in him. Paul writes that God can "fill you with all joy and peace as you trust in him" (Rom. 15:13).

At the Last Supper, shortly before his death on the cross, Jesus spoke with his disciples, telling them he would soon be gone from their presence. Jesus knew they would need encouragement in his absence.

He had just declared his love for them and promised that if they kept his commandments, they would abide in his love.

Then Jesus said to them, "I have told you this so that my joy may be in you and that your joy may be complete" (John 15:11). When the disciples failed to understand his talk about leaving and about resurrection, Jesus explained, "You will rejoice, and no one will take away your joy" (John 16:22).

Having inner divine joy settles a peaceful contentment over us. This joy remains through good times and rough times, in disappointments and frustrations.

The joy of the Lord is like elevator music. It's always there. We can say with the Old Testament prophet, "Do not grieve, for the joy of the LORD is your strength" (Neh. 8:10).

God's joy reflects through us in a personality that is positive, pleasant, sensitive, flexible, and considerate. These traits come from having God's joy, not from a passing happiness.

Do we look forward to getting up each morning? We can, when God's joy fills our heart.

A fruit of the Holy Spirit, joy sweetens every morning, brightens afternoons, and manifests itself in thanksgiving at day's end. With it we can wake up each morning, live our day, and go to sleep at night with joy surrounding us. What a buffer against any problems!

For great is the LORD and most worthy of praise. (Psalm 96:4)

Reliance, Not Understanding

Lean not on your own understanding. (Proverbs 3:5)

M any people teach their children not to question God's decisions and actions in their life. Some of us learned that questioning God shows weak faith.

But when the abused are afraid to seek help for their safety's sake, or when death snatches a parent away from the family in the prime of life, or when cancer and AIDS gain strength in their daily rampage among us, how can we not question and silently cry, "Why, God?"

Wondering whether to question God, I am reassured by these words of Jesus: "My God, My God, why have you forsaken me?" (Matt. 27:46). Even Jesus surrendered to his agony of the cross and uttered, "Why?" Can humankind be less immune to such questioning?

I'm reminded that God sustained Jesus through and beyond the pain of the cross. He lifted his Son from the borrowed grave and now he sits on the heavenly throne at the right hand of God, enjoying uninterrupted fellowship with his Father (Matt. 26:64). In the book of Revelation, Jesus promises if we endure earth's struggles and overcome them he will grant us the same honor and privilege to sit with him on that throne (Rev. 3:21).

Scripture teaches, "Trust in the LORD with all your heart and lean not on your own understanding" (Prov. 3:5). Doing so won't eliminate all difficulties in life. We may still ask, "Why?" But by relying on God, we can hold securely to the knowledge of his help (Ps. 121:2). His mercy and grace are boundless!

I will exalt you, my God the King; I will praise your name for ever and ever. (Psalm 145:1)

God Still Descends

Mount Sinai was covered with smoke, because the Lord descended on it in fire. (Exodus 19:18)

The day our family moved into a new town, my unpacking was interrupted by the sound of the doorbell. Scrambling around boxes piled in the middle of the floor, I hurried to answer it.

I opened the door. A little boy smiled up at me. Before I could ask him what he wanted, he shrugged his small shoulders and said, "Well, here I am!" Apparently, he had waited as long as he could before coming over to see the new people.

Don't we sometimes wish God would announce his presence as matter-of-factly as that little boy on my doorstep? But the truth is that we can know God's presence. He descends to us through our Bible reading, our prayer, and our fellowship with other believers.

I feel God's presence surround me when I join in with other believers to sing praise choruses in worship services. A sweet, sweet spirit from God fills the place.

When I stand aside and watch my grandchildren at play and see their kindness toward one another, I see God in their smiling faces. He created them in his likeness and he is near to me through them.

God visits me in my sickness when he shows his compassion through friends and loved ones who care for me. He reaches down to me even through every medical decision and touch administered to help restore my health.

As I study Scripture and offer my prayers and praise to God, he joins me in my quiet times. He listens to me and refreshes me for each day I must face.

In these and many other ways, God announces, "Well, here I am!"

Sing to God, sing praise to his name. (Psalm 68:4)

Light for the Valleys

Even though I walk through the valley of the shadow of death . . . (Psalm 23:4)

I've read Psalm 23 many times and heard its words repeated on occasions of bereavement. Knowing that "the Lord is my shepherd . . ." (Ps. 23:1) does bring comfort to the listener.

But just what does this "valley of the shadow of death" mean? A minister conducting a funeral made the phrase clearer for me when he explained: "Without light there can be no shadow."

Psalm 23 depicts the journey from life to death as passing through a valley darkened by death's shadow. Beyond death and its shadow lies the reason for that shadow—the light of God. The security of that Light brings victory over death (1 Cor. 15:54–55).

Books have been written about near-death experiences of those medically defined as dead, but who lived to tell about it. A common thread running through most of these experiences is seeing a bright light at the end of a tunnel. Those who recount their experiences never quite reached the light. Many near-death survivors believe God was the source of that light; indeed, he was that light.

Revelation 21:23 describes the future holy city, New Jerusalem: "The city does not need the sun or the moon to shine in it, for the glory of God gives it light, and the Lamb is its lamp."

But, wait! This divine light is present and available this side of death's valley as well. God's word can light our journey through life's valleys: "Your word is a lamp to my feet and a light for my path" (Ps. 119:105). Our steps can be sure when we apply the advice which Isaiah gave to the house of Jacob and "walk in the light of the Lord" (Isa. 2:5).

Jesus urges people to walk in the light so that darkness will not overtake them. If we walk in darkness, Jesus says, we don't know where we're going (John 12:35). He says, "I have come into the world as a light, so that no one who believes in me should stay in darkness" (John 12:46).

If you are stumbling along in disobedience, let God flood the avenues of your life with his light.

Were you brought up in a Christian home only to turn away from the light? Are you determined to self-destruct by choosing Satan as your master, rejecting all your Christian principles? Have you walked willingly into Satan's dark valleys of immorality, idolatry, selfishness, and envy, and find yourself bent low in sin's inky shadows?

I watched a friend take this route. When Satan's hold seemed permanent, my friend finally prayed for a way out. God was waiting and stretched out his rescuing hand.

We can claim victory through life's dark valleys. We can move beyond the shadow into the marvelous light of his face (Psalm 4:6)!

Let them praise the name of the LORD, for his name alone is exalted; his splendor is above the earth and the heavens. (Psalm 148:13)

Where Are We Looking?

"But seek his kingdom, and these things will be given to you as well." (Luke 12:31)

What holds our attention most? A new car? A bigger house? Better clothes? College for the kids? A vacation?

Jesus says if we will seek his kingdom, what we *need* will be given to us as well (Luke 12:27–31).

After feeding the five thousand, Jesus urged his disciples to go by boat to the other side of the lake (Matt. 14:22–31). Dismissing the crowd, Jesus went off alone to pray.

His prayer time finished, Jesus went to rejoin the disciples. But their boat had already moved a great distance from shore, stormy winds blowing it about.

Jesus walked across the water to reach the disciples' boat. Fear overcame them when they saw someone walking on the water. Jesus identified himself, reassuring them in their terror. But Peter wanted personal proof that it was Jesus.

Peter challenged. "Lord, if it's you . . . tell me to come to you on the water" (Matt. 14:28).

Jesus replied simply, "Come" (v. 29).

When Peter climbed from the boat, he successfully walked on the water toward Jesus. Looking about Peter saw the strong wind. Then he became afraid and began to sink.

Catching Peter, Jesus says, "You of little faith . . . why did you doubt?" (v. 31). Peter had it all going well, but he took his eyes off Jesus, more concerned about the wind.

Where are we looking?

The LORD reigns, he is robed in majesty; the LORD is robed in majesty and is armed with strength. (Psalm 93:1)

Thank-you Notes

Let us come before him with thanksgiving. (Psalm 95:2)

The last time pizza arrived at our door, did we thank the delivery person? When that teenager helped get our groceries to the car, did we say thank you? When the neighbors returned our stray pet or gave us mail delivered to them by mistake, did we express thanks? Probably. Most of us voice such appreciation automatically.

Polite manners demand a gracious thank-you to even the most casual dinner host. Can we be any less mannerly toward God who supplies us much more abundantly?

All the blessings we enjoy come from God (James 1:17). It's easy to grumble, even to God, about the undesirable things in our lives. But when we concentrate on those negative things, we lose sight of the many good things in our daily lives, taking them for granted.

Following biblical examples, let's not forget to offer thanksgiving to God. Even Jesus thanked God for hearing his prayers (John 11:41). Have we thanked God for hearing ours? Although God invites us to bring him our needs, we're also to offer him thanksgiving (Phil. 4:6; Col. 4:2).

The apostle Paul thanked God for his gift of salvation through Jesus Christ (2 Cor. 9:15). In 1 Thessalonians 2:13, Paul thanked God for changed lives of those who believed in him.

In addition to answered prayer, salvation, and changed lives, do we have something to thank God for? Paul was thankful for the strength which enabled him to perform in the ministry of Jesus Christ his Lord (1 Tim. 1:12).

Ability for all we do comes from God (2 Cor. 3:5). What ability can we thank God for giving us? Perhaps it's as small a thing as reading this page or reading the Bible.

Thanksgiving is heaven's theme: "Thanks and honor and power and strength be to our God for ever and ever" (Rev. 7:12). It is God's will that we be thankful to him (1 Thess. 5:18). Always give "thanks to God the Father for everything, in the name of our Lord Jesus Christ" (Eph. 5:20).

Praise the LORD. *Praise the* LORD *from the heavens, praise him in the heights above. (Psalm 148:1)*

A Permanent Sign

"This is the sign of the covenant . . . between me and all life on the earth." (Genesis 9:17)

Only a reckless driver ignores a stop sign. A blinking yellow traffic light gets our attention, and we drive with caution through an intersection. We don't challenge "Beware of the Dog" warnings on fences. From sad experience, we usually pay attention to signs.

God rewarded Noah's faith by promising him never again to destroy humankind with flood waters. God sealed the covenant with a sign that all future generations would recognize, a sign that would signify God's faithfulness to keep his word.

God's rainbow is a timeless thing of beauty for all peoples. It bridges cultures and politics.

We're still under that same covenant today. Whenever we see a rainbow spanning the sky, we can know God's word is permanent and true. Only God could form those ribbons of brilliant hues and stretch them across the sky in perfect harmony.

While visiting Hawaii, I was thrilled to see rainbows dot the vast Pacific skies daily. As the frequent rain showers moved across the islands, a misty rainbow soon followed. How refreshing to look toward the mountains and see the sign of God's promise to all humankind. Stretched across the sky, God's rainbow completed the tropical paradise, a setting to surely rival any part of his magnificent creation.

Only God would seal a promise with such beauty. What a reminder of the permanence and truth of God's word! What a mighty God we serve!

From the rising of the sun to the place where it sets, the name of the LORD is to be praised. (Psalm 113:3)

By the Sea

"Therefore everyone who hears these words of mine and puts them into practice is like a wise man who built his house on the rock." (Matthew 7:24)

I sat reading in the round shade of a yellow beach umbrella when motion out of the corner of my eye grabbed my attention. But when I looked, I saw nothing.

I'd picked my spot on the beach a good distance back from the water. Some people set their chairs right at the edge, letting waves lap across their feet. That's not my kind of fun. I don't grant any sea creature—large of small—the chance to nip at my toes.

In spite of my safe location, I became jumpy when something moved in the sand near me.

Trying to forget what obviously wasn't there, I went back to my reading. Before long, another movement caught my eye. I played this hide-and-seek game for several minutes: Something moving, me searching, nothing there.

After turning my chair to a different angle, I pretended to read while looking over the top edge of my book toward my predator's territory. I'd catch him now.

There! I saw the sand move. But I didn't see anything which had caused it. All I spotted was a small measure of sand crumbling from the crest of a deep footprint.

I removed my sunglasses for a clearer look. It happened again: More sand changed position. As I scanned other nearby areas of the beach I saw similar activity every several minutes all around me.

I realized this probably was occurring over the entire beach—grains of sand shifting before my eyes. I wondered if the beach ever remained the same from minute to minute.

With the sand moving continually, however small the amount, I concluded that the beach's structure would change every day.

Then I recalled Jesus teaching about building a house on solid foundation (Matt. 7:24–27). The truth of his parable came through to me like an unexpected thunderclap.

Sand *did* shift. Anything resting on it would have to shift.

That's what Jesus wanted me to learn: He is the constant footing of my faith. He'd spoken this lesson with simple illustration, but until that moment I hadn't grasped his whole truth.

I had believed his words and never doubted the message. Now I had proof of how silly I'd be to expect shifting sand to afford a steady base for anything. I wouldn't think of building my home on such a shallow promise of strength. Why, then, would I refuse Jesus as the solid core of my life?

Praise the Lord, all his works everywhere in his dominion. (Psalm 103:22)

In Over Our Heads

Let us then approach the throne of grace with confidence, so that we may receive mercy and find grace to help us in our time of need. (Hebrews 4:16)

A child's shrill voice disturbed my catnap at poolside one vacation afternoon. Blinking against the sun, I discovered a little girl of five or six perched on the diving board. I watched as she advanced a step or two toward the board's end, then turned around and eased back, away from the water.

In the pool, her daddy treaded water, gently persuading the child to jump from the board. "Jump close to me," he said.

His daughter ventured forward again, then stopped. "But, Daddy," she pleaded, "I've never jumped without my life preserver. I'll go to the bottom."

"No, you won't," he said. "I'll catch you. Just jump close to me." The little girl took her daddy at his word and jumped almost on top of him. She was all smiles and splashes as they hugged.

What reassurance this father gave to his child!

That's exactly what God gives us—generous reassurance every time we find ourselves in over our heads without a life preserver! When we're tempted, God will help us overcome (1 Cor. 10:13). He will combat our loneliness (Ps. 23; Deut. 31:8). In suffering, his grace will strengthen us (2 Cor. 12:8–10). When we're weary, he will give us rest (Matt. 11:28–29).

Like the little girl on the diving board, we can trust our Heavenly Father's words. He will never forsake us. He is worthy of our praise and thanksgiving!

The voice of the LORD is powerful; the voice of the LORD is majestic. (Psalm 29:4)

Praise the LORD, all you nations; extol him, all you peoples. For great is his love toward us, and the faithfulness of the LORD endures forever. Praise the LORD. (Psalm 117)

To him who is able to keep you from falling and to present you before his glorious presence without fault and with great joy—to the only God our Savior be glory, majesty, power and authority, through Jesus Christ our Lord, before all ages, now and forevermore! Amen. (Jude 24–25)